The Year I Was Born

1992

**Compiled by
Alison Graham**

Illustrated with photographs and drawings by Michael Evans

SIGNPOST BOOKS

The Year I Was Born
1992

SIGNPOST BOOKS
Durdle Door, Littledown, Shaftesbury, Dorset SP7 9HD

Published by Signpost Books Ltd

First published 1997
8 7 6 5 4 3 2

Based on an original idea by Sally Wood
Conceived, designed and produced by Signpost Books Ltd, 1997
Copyright in this format © 1997 Signpost Books Ltd

Text copyright © 1997 Alison Graham
Illustrations copyright © 1997 Michael Evans

Editor: Dorothy Wood
Designer: Carol Marsh

Acknowledgements: Mirror Group Newspapers Ltd. for all the pictures in which they hold copyright,
and Hugh Gallacher for his invaluable help in retrieving them from the files.

ISBN 1 874785 13 9

Colour separations by Fotographics Ltd
Printed and bound in Belgium by Proost Book Production

Front cover photographs:

Clockwise from the top:

Nigel Mansell wins the World Championship

Macaulay Culkin as Kevin in Home Alone 2

Gaby Roslin & Paula Yates on 'The Big Breakfast'

John Major & Screaming Lord Sutch

The Winter Olympics

Sally Gunnell with her gold medal

Centre top:
Dustin Hoffman as Hook

Centre below:
Windsor Castle fire

Back cover photographs:

Left to right: *Mel Gibson*

Campaigning for women priests

Bob sleigh in the Winter Olympics

Freddie Mercury memorial concert

Linford Christie winning the gold in the 100m at the Barcelona Olympics

We're barn owls

January

Engagement announced of Lady Helen Windsor · To the South Pole by Motorbike · Upswing in Reliant Robin Sales

Wednesday January 1

92 Bank Holiday

92 60,000 revellers see in the new year in Trafalgar Square.

92 John McCarthy, Brian Keenan and Terry Waite, who were all held hostage in the Lebanon and released last year, are awarded CBEs, and footballer Gary Lineker is awarded the OBE in the New Year's Honours List.

Thursday January 2

92 Listeners to BBC Radio Newcastle vote Paul 'Gazza' Gascoigne the country's biggest bore, ahead of Jeremy Beadle and Cilla Black.

92 Cody the bison, who appeared in Kevin Costner's award winning film *Dances with Wolves*, has been signed by the Walt Disney Organization to appear in a Wild West show.

Friday January 3

92 Mongolia issues a set of stamps today featuring Fred, Wilma and Pebbles Flintstone, Bang and Betty Rubble and son Ban-Ban. The stamps have been designed by a Mongolian artist.

Saturday January 4

92 ███████

92 The world's most famous steeple chaser, *Red Rum* (27), who competed

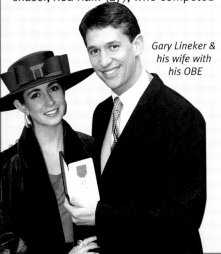

Gary Lineker & his wife with his OBE

in five Grand Nationals, won three and was second twice, is seriously ill.

92 Ariadne, a poisonous Guatemalan bird-eating spider, has been stolen from a house in Forest Hill, London. Police warn that a single bite can paralyse a human adult for up to 10hrs.

Sunday January 5

92 Members of the Swindon Sub Acqua Club take their annual 7.24km swim along the river Thames from Kelmscot to Radcot, Oxon.

92 139 countries in the world now have television. There isn't a single second of the day when *Dr Who* isn't playing somewhere in American.

Monday January 6

92 AT&T (the American Telegraph & Telephone Co) unveil a £1,250 telephone that can send moving pictures of callers as well as their voices.

Tuesday January 7

92 West Middlesex Hospital, London, is trying to discover why in the last 4 months it has received linen from 68 hospitals, including one in New York, as well as hundreds of pillow cases from a shipping line.

Wednesday January 8

92 Lady Helen Windsor (26), daughter of the Duke and Duchess of Kent, announces her engagement to fellow art dealer Tim Taylor (28).

92 Derbyshire is using narrower white lines for road markings in an effort to save money.

Thursday January 9

92 19,895 tail waggers converge on the NEC Birmingham where Crufts Dog Show opens today.

92 There is 150mm of snow in mid Wales.

92 The RSPB launch a campaign to save barn owls. There are only 5,000 breeding pairs left.

Friday January 10

92 The Royal Navy is to sell 200 surplus ship's bells including that of *HMS Broningham*, a former command of the Prince of Wales.

92 A 2.26kg car bomb explodes in Whitehall Place, 274m from Downing Street.

Saturday January 11

92 Algeria's Hassiba Boulmerka, the world 1,500m champion, has been denounced by Muslim fundamentalists in her own country for running with naked legs in front of hundreds of men.

Sunday January 12

92 A whippet, Penclose Dutch Gold, owned by Morag Bolton from Kilmarnock wins the Best of Show at Crufts.

92 Nichelle Nichols (55) who plays Lt Uhura in Star Trek, gets her star installed on the Hollywood Walk of Fame.

Monday January 13

92 The tomb and last home of author Robert Louis Stevenson on Mount Vaca, Western Samoa, which is also the official residence of the head of state, is to become a tourist attraction.

Tuesday January 14

92 Warren Beatty *Bugsy Malone*, Nick Nolte *Prince of Tides*, and Anthony Hopkins *Silence of the Lambs* are favourites for the Best Actor award at the Academy Awards. Jodie Foster *Silence of the Lambs* is favourite for the Best Actress.

Wednesday January 15

92 Actress Julia Roberts is nominated Worst-dressed Woman of the Year, followed by Tyne Daly, Jodie Foster, Carly Simon, Faye Dunaway, Kathy Bates, Jane Seymour and Dame Edna Everage.

Thursday, January 16

92 A US space agency observatory in Atlanta, Georgia, has detected 3 quasars between 10-20 billion light years from earth near the Crab Nebula. They are emitting gamma rays whose energy is estimated to be 10-100 million times greater than that of the entire milky way.

Friday January 17

92 A 19th century golf ball made from gutta percha rubber - the missing link between the former feather-filled ball and the modern version - fetches more than £6,000 at an auction in Chester.

Saturday January 18

92 McDonalds wins over the residents of Hampstead. After 11yrs, Camden Council has withdrawn its opposition to McDonalds opening in the High Street.

Sunday January 19

92

92 At the Golden Globe Awards Warren Beatty wins the Best Picture award for *Bugsy Malone*, Nick Nolte Best Actor for *Prince of Tides*, and Jodie Foster Best Actress for *Silence of the Lambs*.

Monday January 20

92 The New Forest is to become a National Park.

92 Steeple chaser *Red Rum* takes a stroll around his Chester stables. Only 3 weeks ago the 27yr-old horse was so ill he was unable to move.

Tuesday January 21

92 Paul McCartney wins the first Royal Swedish Music Academy's Polar Music Prize worth about £110,000. He pledges to give it all away.

92 Thousands of dolphins worldwide are being killed by a viral epidemic and toxic waste.

Wednesday January 22

92 Japanese adventurer Shinji Kazama (44) becomes the first man to reach the South Pole by motorbike, just 5yrs after he reached the North Pole.

Thursday January 23

92 Michael Tan (7) of Wellington, NZ has qualified for a university place by passing New Zealand's bursary mathematics exam, but has decided not to take it up.

Friday January 24

92 The BBC raises £98,875 by selling old TV costumes.

92 Freddie Bartholomew, the famous child star of *Little Lord Fauntleroy* and many other films, dies in Hollywood, aged 67.

Saturday January 25

92 The RSPB is fighting the EC over its backing of Greece to redirect the Archeleos river to the opposite side of the country as some of Europe's rarest species of bird would disappear.

92 Snow in Spain blankets orange groves and beaches as far south as Alicante.

Sunday January 26

My Goodness Bradman's Hit Him For Six

92 Prime Minister John Major appears on the BBC's *Desert Island Discs* to celebrate its 50th anniversary. Amongst his ten choices are *Rhapsody in Blue*; the mad scene from *Lucia de Lammermuir*, and John Arlott's cricket commentary on Don Bradman's final innings in 1948.

Monday January 27

92 People in Britain spent £64 billion on sweets last year - and the average person ate 14kg! We consumed 500,000 tonnes of chocolate, and 300,000 tonnes of mints, liquorice and toffee.

Tuesday January 28

92 Reliant (Robin) 3-wheeler car sales are booming because they are cheap to run, but mainly because Del Boy and Rodney drive one in the TV programme *Only Fools and Horses*.

Wednesday January 29

92 Kathryn Barnes (3) of Ipswich, has become a member of Mensa, the organisation for people with IQs over 148.

92 A helium gas balloon called Earthworks, taller than the Statue of Liberty, is about to take off from Akron, Ohio, USA to attempt the first circumnavigation of the world in a single flight.

Thursday January 30

92 An exhibition in London reveals that when the Queen travels her baggage includes pine-scented soap, barley sugar, white gloves, a set of black mourning clothes, Earl Grey tea and Harrods pork sausages.

92 Charles Dickens is to replace Florence Nightingale on the new £10 when it is issued on April 29.

Friday January 31

92 The village of Spraxton, nr Bridgewater, Somerset, is left £1.5 million by bachelor farmer Bill Geen. He has left £100,000 to the village hall; £25,000 to two churches; £20,000 to the cricket team; £6,000 to the football team. The rest is shared amongst other village organisations, friends, charities and distant relatives.

February

The last mouse-eared bat in Britain is dead · It is the 40th Anniversary of the Queen's reign · Opening of Winter Olympics

Saturday February 1

❄ Millionaire John Paul Getty Jnr is to finance a new home at Hereford Cathedral for the Mappa Mundi.

❄ McDonalds in Moscow has been dubbed the slowest fast food restaurant in the world because of the queues.

Sunday February 2

❄ Priscilla Tolkien unveils a plaque at Bloemfontein Cathedral, South Africa to her father J.R.R. Tolkien, author of *The Hobbit* and *The Lord of the Rings* to celebrate the centenary of his birth *(Jan 3, 1892)*.

❄ Scientists date the body of the iceman found in the Austrian Tyrol last year as that of a man who died in 3500BC.

Monday February 3

❄ ███████████

❄ About 500 Bewick swans at Slimbridge, Glos., are to have their bottoms painted yellow so that birdwatchers can track them to their breeding grounds in Siberia.

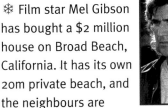

Tuesday February 4

❄ Six people raise £1,000 for a children's ward at Nottingham City Hospital by spending last night at Bottesford Airfield, said to be haunted by World War II airmen.

❄ Film star Mel Gibson has bought a $2 million house on Broad Beach, California. It has its own 20m private beach, and the neighbours are Danny deVito, Steven Spielberg, Goldie Hawn and Sylvester Stallone.

Wednesday February 5

❄ The last-known mouse-eared bat in Britain has been declared dead. No one has seen it in its home in a disused tunnel between Chichester and Midhurst, W Sussex for 2yrs.

Thursday February 6

❄ It is the 40th anniversary of the Queen's accession to the throne.

❄ Actor Sean Connery (James Bond) who has joined the Newington (Edinburgh) branch of the Scottish Nationalist Party, has been given the membership number 007.

Friday February 7

❄ Three Weymouth fishermen summon help with a mobile phone when their ship's radio fails, and are winched to safety by a RN helicopter.

❄ Emmenthal cheese will lose its 'h' in France, to conform with the spelling in every other country.

Saturday February 8

❄ Opening of the Winter Olympics in Albertville, France. The Olympic flame is lit by skier Nathalie Bouvier (22), who broke both legs in a world cup race in Japan last year and cannot compete.

Sunday February 9

❄ Start of Chinese New Year. It is the year of the Monkey.

❄ Two Spaniards Tomas Feliu, an engineer, and Jesus Gonzales Green, a TV journalist, take off from the Canary Is in a hot air balloon to retrace Christopher Columbus's voyage of discovery to America.

Monday February 10

❄ A team from Birmingham University wins the £10,000 Toshiba Year of Invention award for a tiny instrument that is used for on-the-spot blood and urine tests. Amongst more than 4000 inventions submitted, were a self-correcting pen, and an electronically controlled mirror for budgies.

Tuesday February 11

❄ An 2.4m conger eel weighing 55.7kg is caught off Scarborough and landed at Whitby beating the biggest (50.05kg) in the *Guinness Book of Records*.

❄ Channel Islanders are the cleanest people in Britain; 83% take a shower every day and 50% also take a bath several times a week.

Wednesday February 12

❄ Konishiki (28) a champion heavyweight Sumo wrestler, known as the Dump Truck and weighing 260kg, marries former model Sumika Shioda in Tokyo. He is said to be five times heavier than his bride. *(see below)*

Thursday February 13

❄ The Atomic Energy Authority is giving £150,000 worth of protective clothing to workers clearing up the site of the Chernobyl nuclear reactor disaster in the Ukraine.

Friday February 14

❄ St Valentine's Day.

❄ A letter left on the ice in a cigarette tin marked London, and written by T Griffith-Taylor, one of Captain Scott's ill-fated expedition to the South Pole 80yrs ago, has been found in the Antarctic.

❄ California is hit by the worst storms for 100 years. Hundreds are made homeless.

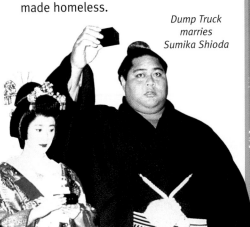

Dump Truck marries Sumika Shioda

UK Fact File • MCMLXXXXII

Total area of the United Kingdom	244,100 sq kms
Capital City	London (1,580 sq kms)
Population of UK	58,006,500
Births	781,017
	400,337 male • 380,680 female
Marriages	356,000
Deaths	634,200
Divorces	175,100
Most popular girl's name*	Emily
Most popular boy's name*	James
Prime Minister	John Major

Head of State	Queen Elizabeth II

Poet Laureate	Edward (Ted) Hughes
Astronomer Royal	Professor Arnold Wolfendale
Royal Swan Keeper	FJ Turk
Royal Barge Masteer	R. Crouch
Archbishop of Canterbury	Dr George Carey
Presidency of EC	Jan-June • Portugal
	July-Dec • Great Britain
Members of EC	Belgium • Denmark • France
	Federal Republic of Germany
	Greece • Ireland • Italy
	Luxembourg • The Netherlands
	Portugal • Spain
	The United Kingdom

* according to The Times newspaper

TOP TOYS

1. WWF wrestlers
2. Trolls
3. Barbie *(particularly Ultra hair)*
4. Sylvanian families
5. Electronic learning aids
6. Lego-Technic propeller plane
7. Polly Pocket
8. Boglins
9. Terminators
10. Sindy *(particularly Dream Ballet doll)*

TOP TOYS OF THE DECADE

1980-81	Rubik's Cube
1982	Star Wars
1983-84	Master of the Universe
1985-86	Transformers
1987-89	Sylvanian Families
1990	Teenage Mutant Turtles
1991	Nintendo Game Boy

TOP TEN NAMES*

	GIRLS	BOYS
1	Emily	James
2	Charlotte	Alexander
3	Olivia	Thomas
4	Sophie	William
5	Lucy	Edward
6	Emma	Charles
7	Sarah	Oliver
8	Georgina	George
9	Alice	Henry
10	Hannah	Samuel

The Top Ten stately homes in Britain last year were:

1. Warwick Castle
2. Blenheim
3. Chatsworth
4. Hever Castle
5. Castle Howard
6. Harwood House
7. Blair Castle
8. Longleat
9. Arundel Castle
10. Bowood House

Saturday February 15

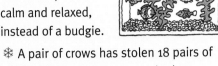

❊ Railway signalmen at Gateshead, Tyne & Wear, have chosen to have an aquarium in the signal box to keep them calm and relaxed, instead of a budgie.

❊ A pair of crows has stolen 18 pairs of windscreen wipers from cars in the car park at the ICI Wilton Works, Teeside.

Sunday February 16

L to R: The Santa Maria, Piñta and the Niña

❊ A Spanish replica of Christopher Columbus's flotilla of 1492 sails into a rapturous welcome in Miami, Florida, the first of 20 ports of call. The Niña, the Piñta and the Santa Maria are escorted into port by thousands of small boats.

Monday February 17

❊ An earthquake measuring 3.3 on the Richter scale shakes Peterborough. The tremor lasts for 50secs.

❊ Nominations for the Golden Raspberry awards for the worst performances in films include Sean Young and Demi Moore in the worst actress category. Demi's husband Bruce Willis is nominated as worst actor for his role in Hudson Hawk.

Tuesday February 18

❊ US pop group New Kids on the Block leave Korea. Their last concert in Seoul was interrupted for 3 1/2hrs when screaming, frenzied fans stormed the stage.

❊ Uproar in Australia when the prime minister's wife, Annita Keating, declines to curtsey when greeting the Queen and the Duke of Edinburgh at the start of their 7 day tour.

Wednesday February 19

❊ The Queen marks Sydney's 150th anniversary at a ceremony in Town Hall Square.

❊ Students at the 'women only' Somerville College, Oxford, protest against the admission of men to the college.

Thursday February 20

❊ The Queen opens the Australian parliament. Two republican members of the Labor party boycott the opening. 52% of Australians support the idea of an Australian Head of State.

Friday February 21

❊ Skater Kristi Yamaguchi (USA) wins the gold medal at the Olympic Games in Albertville.

❊ Michael Jackson, in London with his cousin Brett (10), goes on a shopping spree, spending more than £2,000 on toys in Hamleys, Regent Street.

Saturday February 22

❊ Jean Calmet, believed to be the world's oldest person, celebrates her 117th birthday in Arles, France with cake and champagne.

Sunday February 23

❊ Twitchers get excited by the sighting of a rare grey gyr falcon from the Arctic on the Isle of Sheppey. A white gyr falcon is also spotted on the Shetland island of Fetlar.

❊ At the Winter Olympics at Albertville, France, Germany tops the table with 26 medals

Monday February 24

❊ Chris Lowe of the Pet Shop Boys, buys Fabden's Park, a 15th century house at Cold Christmas, Herefordshire, for £1m.

❊ Heavy snow in Greece - more than 300 mainland and island villages are cut off without phones or electricity

Tuesday February 25

❊ Hula hoops, which swept the USA and UK in the 1950s, are all the rage in Peking, as part of the trend to keep fit and slim. (see below)

❊ Russian scientists believe that the hairy mammoth died out because of a shortage of the mineral salts which wild animals need to balance the salt in their bodies.

Wednesday February 26

❊ At the Grammy Awards Nathalie Cole wins 3 Grammys for Unforgettable, her tribute to her father Nat King Cole; Barbra Streisand gets the lifetime achievement Grammy; Bonnie Rait wins best solo rock vocal performance, and Michael Bolton best male pop performance.

Thursday February 27

❊ Film star Elizabeth Taylor celebrates her 60th birthday in style by taking over Disneyland at Anaheim, USA, and inviting more than a 1000 guests to join the celebrations.

Friday February 28

❊ Next week's concert by Paula Abdul in S Korea will not be open to unaccompanied teenagers after the riots at the New Kids on the Block concert in Seoul last week.

Saturday February 29 - it's leap year.

❊ A Soviet space capsule is on sale in the catalogue of a Paris auction house. It is a descent module of the Photon Satellite, was in orbit for 16 days, and is expected to make 1 million francs.

Hula hoops fifties style

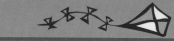

March

I'm a sturgeon

Sir Clive Sinclair unveils the Zike • Duke and Duchess of York separate • Bafta Awards

Sunday March 1

Nigel Mansell driving a Williams wins the South African Grand Prix.

One of L.S. Lowery's best-known paintings, VE DAY 1945, has been stolen from Kelvingrove Gallery, Glasgow during a charity ball.

Traffic chaos on the M4 as the road is blocked by the 79m long 2000 tonne Ingst Road Bridge. It collapses the wheels of the computerised multi-wheeled transporter that was to move it to a layby in Aust for demolition.

Monday March 2

British shoe designers think they have found a way to turn waste fish skins into hide suitable for footwear. It takes four salmon skins per pair of shoes.

Freddie the bottle-nose dolphin who singlehandedly transformed Amble, Northumbs, into a tourist attraction, has left after 5yrs in residence.

Tuesday March 3

Shrove Tuesday.

Guys becomes the London hospital for gourmets as top cook Caroline Waldegrave introduces a new 89p menu.

Racehorse trainer, Martin Pipe, gives his horses polo mints as a treat. He has ordered 168 boxes (one for each horse) for the Cheltenham races.

Wednesday March 4

~~xxxxxxx~~

The Queen is sitting for two Russian artists, Leonid Efros and Alexei Maximov, who are painting miniatures for the Kremlin Armoury.

Richmond Park, London, becomes a site of special scientific interest.

Thursday March 5

Sir Clive Sinclair unveils his new bicycle, part pedal power and part battery and called the Zike, at the Cycling and Outdoor Activities Show at Olympia.

England beat Australia in the Cricket World Cup by 8 wickets.

The BBC buys back Noddy and Big Ears and plans to relaunch them in the autumn.

Friday March 6

The Michelangelo computer virus causes worldwide panic.

Mimine the cat is reunited with his owner, Bertrand, who left him in Turcoing in N. France in 1990 when he went on holiday to Normandy. The cat followed, taking 2yrs to cover the 402km.

Saturday March 7

Richard Branson is £560 million better off today having sold the Virgin Music Group to Thorn EMI.

Sunday March 8

International Womens Day.

Two shrunken heads are sold for £23,000 in a Portsmouth, NH, USA, auction of Indian artefacts. They are bought by the Ripley's Believe it or Not Museum collection.

Monday March 9

Commonwealth Day.

A sturgeon is netted off Weymouth for the first time since 1907. It is offered to the Queen as custom demands, and is in quarantine at Weymouth Sea Life centre until she decides otherwise.

Tuesday March 10

A bomb on the line nr Wandsworth Bridge, London knocks out the signal box; rail services will be disrupted for days.

French climber Catherine Destiville (32) becomes the first woman to climb the 3692m north face of the Eiger solo. It takes her 7hrs.

Wednesday March 11

National No-Smoking Day.

Prime Minister John Major calls a General Election for April 9.

Martin Buser of Switzerland, who sings to his dogs, wins the 1866km Iditarod Trail dog sled race across Alaska. He is 10hrs ahead of his nearest rival, and breaks the previous record by 6hrs.

Thursday March 12

John McCarthy, Terry Waite and Brian Keenan receive their CBEs at Buckingham Palace.

The Hula Hoop craze is so enormous in China, that there are six factories in Peking each producing 10,000 a day.

Friday March 13

Sidney Poitier (68) becomes the first black actor to receive the Life Achievement Award of the American Film Institute.

An earthquake in Eastern Turkey measures between 6.2 and 6.8 on the Richter Scale causing hundreds of deaths.

Saturday March 14

Bill Oddie, star of the Goodies and well-known bird watcher, is spearheading a campaign by Norfolk police to catch people who steal eggs.

A second earthquake rocks Eastern Turkey.

Sunday March 15

A Soyuz rocket will be launched next week to rescue Sergei Krikalev, who has been marooned in the *Mir* space station for over ten months because of a lack of funds to launch a rescue mission.

Monday March 16

Graham Cross (15) from Walsall, W Midlands, who is named after the entire Manchester United 1977 FA Cup winning team, signs schoolboy terms for Leeds.

Hairy potatoes could be on the menu soon. Scientists in Peru have crossed a wild potato with a hairy skin with a standard potato. It is very good at repelling disease and insects, and tastes good.

Tuesday March 17

A Soyuz TM14 rocket blasts off from the Baikonur launch site, Kazakhstan, to rescue Sergei Krikalev and Alexandr Volnov from the orbiting *Mir* space station.

Wednesday March 18

Two instruments built by Antonio Stradivari in the 1690s fetch nearly £1 million at Christie's sale. The 'Bonjour' violoncello sells for £605,00 and the 'Schreiber' violin for £352,000.

Thursday March 19

Buckingham Palace announces that the Duke and Duchess of York are to separate.

South African voters give Mr de Klerk an overwhelming mandate to go ahead and negotiate power sharing with the black majority.

Friday March 20

Soyuz TM14 docks with the *Mir* space station.

At the Broadcasting Press Guild TV and Radio Awards, Helen Mirren *(above)* is named Best Actress of 1991 for *Prime Suspect*, Robert Lindsay Best Actor for *GBH*, Alan Bennet receives the writer's award for *A Question of Attribution* and Alistair Cooke is Radio Broadcaster of the Year.

Saturday March 21

Tower Hamlets Council is offering for sale a 19th century underground public lavatory on a traffic island the size of two tennis courts in Bow Road for £15,000. The entrance to the gents is under a statue of Gladstone, and the ladies in the grounds of nearby Bow Church.

Sunday March 22

England reach the final of the cricket World Cup in Australia.

Nigel Mansell wins the Mexico Grand Prix.

BAFTA awards go to Anthony Hopkins - Best Actor -*Silence of the Lambs*; Alan Parker - Best Director - *The Commitments*; Anthony Minghella - Best Original Screen Play - *Truly, Madly, Deeply*; Alan Rickman - Best Supporting actor - *Robin Hood - Prince of Thieves*; Jodie Foster - Best Actress - *Silence of the Lambs*. Of the TV Awards, *Inspector Morse* wins Best Drama, and *One Foot in the Grave* Best Comedy.

Monday March 23

At the final of the 1992 British Sausage Song Contest, the winner out of 400 entries is a rap number *Bangers* by Cliff Douse. He wins a Yamaha keyboard, a professional recording session, a trophy in the shape of a sausage and a pair of quavers, and a year's supply of sausages.

Tuesday March 24

Astronaut Dr Michael Foale, who was born in Britain, blasts off from Cape Canaveral in the shuttle *Atlantis* on an 8-day mission to examine the effects of the sun on the earth's atmosphere. Helen Sharman, Britain's first astronaut, made her flight in a *Mir* spaceship.

Wednesday March 25

Sergei Krikalev (33) comes back to earth after 313 days in orbit in the *Mir* space station. While he has been in space, the Soviet Union has split up, Mikhail Gorbachev has been replaced by Boris Yeltsin, and the name of his home town has reverted from Leningrad to St Petersburg.

Pakistan beat England in the final of the Cricket World Cup by 22 runs.

Thursday March 26

Planeloads of twitchers descend on Shetland to catch a glimps of the rare pine grosbeak, last seen in Britain 17yrs ago. It usually lives in N Scandinavia and Russia.

Friday March 27

Trading Places Day - to raise money for the Royal Marsden Hospital, London - children take over classes from teachers in schools, Richard Branson serves drinks on one of his planes and, on the election trail, Prime Minister John Major is handed a TV camera and obligingly films the crowd surrounding him.

Saturday March 28

Clocks go forward at 1am. Experts say that tomorrow morning over 3 million people will not know what the time is despite warnings on radio, TV and in the papers.

Sunday March 29

John Anderson (24), up for a spin in a 4-seater aeroplane, safely lands the plane under instruction from another pilot (Robert Legge) flying next to him when his pilot, his father-in-law to be, has a heart attack. He has never flown a plane before.

Monday March 30

Golden Raspberry Night, which precedes the Oscars - *Hudson Hawke* wins the title Worst Film and Kevin Costner is Worst Actor for *Robin Hood Prince of Thieves*.

Silence of the Lambs is the top of the Oscars with Anthony Hopkins and Jodie Foster, winning Best Actor and Best Actress, and Jonathan Demme picking up the prize for Best Director.

Tuesday March 31

Birmingham street sweepers have been asked to search for the head of a £275,000 statue in the city centre. It is thought ot have been knocked off and used as a football by hooligans.

April

Wednesday April 1

🥚 April Fool's Day.

🥚 An enormous parasitic fungus has been discovered in the forests of Michigan, USA. The fungus *Armillaria bulbosa*, grows mainly underground and is estimated to measure at least 150,000 sq m, weigh 100 tonnes and be 1,500 years old.

Thursday April 2

🥚 British-born astronaut Michael Foales returns to earth after more than a week in orbit in the space shuttle *Atlantis*.

🥚 The centre of Venice is flooded after 4 days of heavy rain.

Friday April 3

🥚 ▓▓▓▓▓▓

🥚 Bruce (4) the Australian three-toed Potoroo (kangaroo rat) from Blackpool Zoo, the only male in captivity, is to fly to the Smithsonian Institute, Washington DC, USA, as a potential mate for its two females. In return for Bruce's services, Blackpool hopes to receive a pair of armadillos.

Saturday April 4

🥚 *Party Politics*, ridden by Carl Llewellyn, wins the Grand National at Aintree.

🥚 Oxford beat Cambridge in the 138th boat race by 1 1/4 lengths.

🥚 The Duke of Edinburgh, on a works train, becomes the first royal to travel through the Channel Tunnel.

Sunday April 5

🥚 Nigel Mansell wins the Brazilian Grand Prix, his third successive win.

🥚 Christie's in Amsterdam takes delivery of a 300-year-old cargo of Chinese porcelain recovered from a wreck off the Vietnamese coast, valued at £1.5 million.

Monday April 6

🥚 Britain, which is to be chairman of the EEC in July unveils the logo - Rory the lion.

🥚 Ringo Starr - the former Beatles drummer - launches his first album in 9yrs.

Tuesday April 7

🥚 About 45,000 people have visited the church at Sodertalje, south of Stockholm to be blessed by a 16yr-old girl who claims that Jesus, the Holy Mother and Mar Chabel, the Lebanese saint, have appeared to her in visions.

Wednesday April 8

🥚 The two-day sale at Christie's, Amsterdam, of Chinese porcelain recovered from the wreck off the Vietnamese coast raises £4.1 million.

🥚 Bees are threatened with the deadly parasite varroasis: a 40km exclusion zone is imposed around Okehampton, Devon.

Thursday April 9

🥚 Election Day.

🥚 Scientists at Bergen University, Norway, are asking children worldwide to send them their milk teeth for a pollution study.

🥚 The last-ever issue of *Punch* magazine appears today.

Friday April 10

🥚 The Conservatives win the General Election with an overall majority of 21 seats.

🥚 An IRA bomb at the Baltic Exchange in the City of London, causes widespread damage. Another bomb at Staples Corner damages the A5 flyover.

Saturday April 11

🥚 Sergei Krikalev (34) the cosmonaut who spent 10 months on a *Mir* space station, is made a Hero of the Russian Federation.

Sunday April 12

🥚 Palm Sunday.

🥚 The London Marathon is won by Antonio Pinto of Portugal and Katrin Dorre of Germany.

🥚 A tide of white-hot lava, 100m wide, slithers slowly down Mt Etna, Sicily, towards the town of Zafferana.

🥚 Mickey Mouse officially opens Euro Disney in Paris. Saboteurs blow up an electricity pylon hours before the opening, but Disney's $10 million party goes ahead on emergency power!

Monday April 13

🥚 Neil Kinnock resigns as leader of the Labour Party.

🥚 A 30sec earthquake in Bonn, Germany, measures 5.5-5.8 on the Richter scale, the biggest in N Europe this century.

Tuesday April 14

🥚 Treasure hunters in Montevideo, Uruguay, led by Argentine oceanographer Ruben Collado, recover gold coins and ingots worth £565,000 from *El Preciado*, a Spanish galleon that sank in the River Plate in 1792.

Wednesday April 15

🥚 A team of Cambridge archaeologists has found the entrance to the ancient port of Carthage which silted up 13 centuries ago.

🥚 Lava from Mt Etna has almost reached the town of Zafferana, Sicily.

🥚 Musical maestro Andrew Lloyd Webber pays £10.5 million for Canaletto's *View of the Old Horse Guards, London*.

Thursday April 16

🥚 Queen's *Bohemian Rhapsody* wins the Ivor Novello award for the best-selling record of last year.

1992

BRIT AWARDS (Feb 12)

Queen	**Best Single** - *These are the Days of Our Lives.*
Seal	*3 awards* - **Best Male Artist, Best Album, Best Video.**
Lisa Stansfield	**Best Female Artist**
KLF and Simply Red	*tied* **Best British Group**
Trevor Horn	**Best Producer**
Beverley Craven	**Best British Newcomer**
Prince	**Best International Artist**
REM	**Best International Group**
PM Dawn	**Best International Newcomer**
The Commitments	**Best Soundtrack**

KLF

PM Dawn

Mick Hucknall

Beverley Craven

Seal

Lisa Stansfield

Queen

Prince

The Commitments

REM

Michael Jackson

Jimmy Nail

Snap

Lionel Richie

Whitney Houston

Simply Red

Wet Wet Wet

Michael Bolton

Annie Lennox

TOP TEN SINGLES

1	*I Will Always Love You*	**Whitney Houston**
2	*Rhythm is a Dancer*	**Snap**
3	*Would I Lie to You*	**Charles and Eddie**
4	*Stay*	**Shakespeare's Sister**
5	*Please Don't Go*	**KWS**
6	*End of the Road*	**Boys to Men**
7	*Abba-Esque*	**EP**
8	*Ain't No Doubt*	**Jimmy Nail**
9	*Heal the World*	**Michael Jackson**
10	*Goodnight Girl*	**Wet Wet Wet**

TOP TEN ALBUMS

1	*Simply Red*	**Simply Red**
2	*Back to Front*	**Lionel Richie**
3	*Cher's Greatest Hits 1965-1992*	**Cher**
4	*Glittering Prize 81/92*	**Simple Minds**
5	*Dangerous*	**Michael Jackson**
6	*Diva*	**Annie Lennox**
7	*Timeless the Classics*	**Michael Bolton**
8	*Divine Madness*	**Madness**
9	*We Can't Dance*	**Genesis**
10	*Up*	**Right Said Fred**

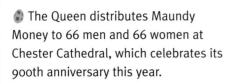

The Queen distributes Maundy Money to 66 men and 66 women at Chester Cathedral, which celebrates its 900th anniversary this year.

Friday April 17

Good Friday

US President George Bush's springer spaniel, Millie, earned more money than the president last year. Royalties from *Millie's Book* - an under-the-table look at the Bush White House - totalled £512,000.

Saturday April 18

650 canoeists from all over the world, take part in the 44th 200km race from Devizes to Westminster.

A 500yr-old fish is found by archaeologists excavating the kitchen area at Mount Grace Priory, a Carthusian monastery nr Northallerton, N Yorks.

Sunday April 19

Easter Sunday

Zafferana in Sicily is swamped with tourists who pick up bits of warm lava from Mt Etna as souvenirs.

A hoard of silver coins thought to have been hidden in the 1480s has been found in a 23cm jug in Selby, Yorks.

Comedian Frankie Howerd (75) dies.

Monday April 20

Bank Holiday.

72,000 fans throng Wembley Stadium for a memorial concert to Freddie Mercury, lead singer of Queen. It is beamed to a TV and radio audience in 70 countries, and is expected to raise £1 million for Aids projects worldwide.

Comedian Bennie Hill (67) dies.

King Juan Carlos and Queen Sophia open Expo 92 in Seville, Spain: 110 countries are taking part.

Tuesday April 21

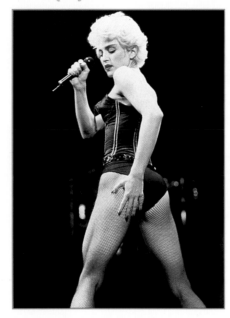

Pop star Madonna signs a deal with Time Warner Inc which makes her the highest paid female entertainer in history.

Wednesday April 22

The PO issues four stamps to commemorate the 350th anniversary of the Battle of Edgehill.

Freddie the dolphin who disappeared from Amble, Northumberland on March 2, has been sighted off Tynemouth.

Thursday April 23

St George's Day

The world's largest McDonalds opens in Peking.

Friday April 24

Mohammad Alam Channa is officially the tallest man in the world at 2.3m. He has size 22 feet, and his hand measures 28cm from the heel of the palm to the tip of the middle finger.

Saturday April 25

The US postal service say that more than 1 million people voted in a postal ballot to select which of 2 pictures of Elvis

Presley would appear on a new stamp. The majority opted for young Elvis.

An earthquake in California measures 6.9 on the Richter scale.

Sunday April 26

At the Olivier Awards, the Best Actor prize goes to Nigel Hawthorne in *The Madness of King George* written by Alan Bennett, who wins two further prizes as Best Actor in a Musical or Entertainment in his own *Talking Heads*, which also wins Outstanding Production of the Year. Best Actress is Juliet Stevenson in *Death and the Maiden*.

Monday April 27

Andrew Lloyd Webber lends his £10.5 million Canaletto to the Tate Gallery, London *(See April 15)*.

A Japanese tourist causes a bomb scare in Reading, Berks, when he leaves his briefcase sporting an Irish flag chained to a bench while he goes shopping.

Tuesday April 28

Betty Boothroyd (62) becomes the 155th and first woman Speaker of the House of Commons by 372 votes to 238.

Painter Francis Bacon dies.

Wednesday April 29

China is to spend £30 million to protect its pandas. The Forestry ministry will set up panda reserves in Sichuan, Gansu and Shaanxi provinces.

The new smaller £10 note is issued.

Thursday April 30

Following a TV programme in Britain, money floods into the Brooke Hospital for Sick Animals in Cairo, which buys old, sick and undernourished animals from their owners for care and treatment.

Blacks riot in Los Angeles when police are cleared of assault on motorist Rodney King.

May

Ireland wins Eurovision Song Contest • PHEW WHAT A SCORCHER. It is the hottest May for 150 years

Friday May 1

Hundreds of Joneses invade Wales for the 'International Jones Day' opening of the Garden Festival Wales at Ebbw Vale.

Saturday May 2

An 11-man French rowing team crosses the Atlantic from the Canary Is. to Martinique in 35days 8hrs, setting a new record.

Surfing beaches around Los Angeles are closed because of the riots in the city over the Rodney King case.

Sunday May 3

Nigel Mansell wins the Spanish Grand Prix in Barcelona, his fourth win in a row.

Jacob Herren (Sw) wins the European Pipe Smokers cup at St Cloud, Jura, France. He takes 52min 11 sec to smoke 1/10th of an ounce of tobacco: the record is more than 3hrs.

Monday May 4

Ten tigers look on as game wardens rescue 4 people from the tiger enclosure at Woburn, Beds., when their Panda car overheats. The car explodes shortly afterwards.

250 twitchers invade the home of Ian and Jane Shedden of Hamilton, nr. Glasgow, to see a dark-eyed Junco - only the 16th ever to be seen in the UK.

Tuesday May 5

The Ninth National Worm Charming championship takes place at Blackawton, Devon. The winners charm just 53 worms - last years winners charmed 65.

England is to host the European Football Championships in 1996.

Famous actress and film star Marlene Dietrich dies at her apartment in Paris.

Wednesday May 6

The State Opening of Parliament.

The TV film of the Prince of Wales's book *The Old Man of Lochnagar*, will be shown in the USA.

Thursday May 7

At Christie's, London, Rock Memorabilia sale, John Lennon's black leather bomber jacket is sold for £24,400; an early Rolling Stones poster fetches £1,000, and Jimi Hendrix's felt hat £4,950.

Friday May 8

Harrison Ford as Indiana Jones, and Vivien Leigh as Scarlett O'Hara top the poll of US filmgoers who were asked which film characters they would most like to be.

Saturday May 9

Liverpool beat Sunderland by 2-0 at Wembley to win the FA Cup for the third time in 6yrs.

Ireland wins the Eurovision Song Contest with *Why Me*? sung by Linda Martin, and composed by Johnny Logan. Britain is second with *One Step at a Time* sung by Michael Ball.

Sunday May 10

On behalf of the Dead Comics Society, Comedian Ernie Wise unveils a plaque to the late, great Tony Hancock on the house in Hampstead Garden Suburb where he lived from 1947-1948.

Monday May 11

The only pair of golden eagles in England and Wales hatch a chick at their eyrie in the Lake District. RSPB

wardens have kept a 24hr a day watch on the nest since the eggs were laid in late March.

Tuesday May 12

Inspector Morse spearheads 20 hours of dubbed British films and videos on television in the CIS. More than 300 million viewers are expected to tune in.

Wednesday May 13

Bracknell Forest Borough Council goes green and replaces its old tractor in the gardening department with two Shire horses.

Postmen will be allowed to wear shorts this summer (Bermuda length or similar) provided the temperature reaches 26°C (78°F).

Thursday May 14

Three US astronauts take a space walk from the *Endeavour* space shuttle 321,728m above Hawaii to capture and repair an Intelsat-VI satellite which has been drifting aimlessly since a booster rocket failed at its launch 2yrs ago.

Welsh (23) the last deep mine pit pony in S Wales, retires to an RSPCA farm nr Milton Keynes.

Blackpool Tower reopens after a £13 million refurbishment.

Friday May 15

Papa Stour in the Shetland Islands broadcasts a radio appeal for more settlers. The population of the island is down to 23 people.

Saturday May 16

President and Mrs Bush kept gifts worth £11,723 last year including 3 bathrobes and 2 sweatshirts from Donald Trump, a briefcase from Dan Aykroyd and 2 porcelain figurines from Chancellor Kohl of Germany.

Sunday May 17

Nigel Mansell wins the San Marino Grand Prix, his fifth win in a row.

The *Endeavour* space shuttle lands safely after completing 4,183,400km, and rescuing the stranded Intelsat-VI satellite. The crew made three space walks.

Monday May 18

A medieval gold ring found in a field at Middleham, N Yorks, will be put on display at the York Museum. The ring sold at auction for £45,980.

Tuesday May 19

Chelsea Flower Show opens

The north stand at Highbury Stadium, home of Arsenal Football Club is demolished, as part of a £20 million redevelopment.

The ancient oak in Sherwood Forest in which Robin Hood is said to have hidden has been cloned in a test-tube so that exact copies will be growing when the old one dies.

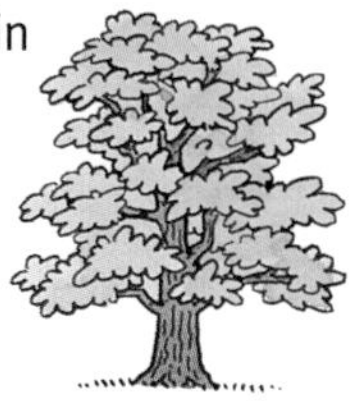

Wednesday May 20

Sue, the biggest fossil of a Tyrannosaurus Rex ever discovered has been seized by the FBI as evidence in an ownership dispute in S Dakota, USA. The skeleton was found in 1990 on a ranch inside the Cheyenne River Sioux tribe's reservation and bought for $5,000.00 by the Institute of Geological Research in S Dakota. The Indians say that the sale was illegal and Sue belongs to the tribe.

Thursday May 21

Guests at the New York Entomological Society Banquet feast on Peppery Delight Mealworm Dip; California Sushi Roll containing waxworms; Cricket Tempura; Mealworm Meatballs; Sauteed Hin Thai Water Bugs in hot sauce and Assorted Insect Sugar Cookies.

Friday May 22

George Preece (100) of Hereford, who has driven for 83yrs with only one minor accident, has been allowed to renew his car insurance for 1p.

Residents of the seaside resort of Frinton, which has no pubs, no amusement arcades, no candy floss stalls and no saucy postcards are horrified by the Copper Kettle Tea Rooms becoming a fish and chip shop.

Saturday May 23

A Florida lorry driver is trapped for 3hrs in his truck after an accident when police have to fight millions of angry bees to get him out. He was transporting 250 hives, each containing about 20,000 bees.

Sunday May 24

Hail, heavy rain and thunderstorms.

Spaghetti Junction, otherwise known as the Gravelly Hill Interchange, Birmingham, is 20yrs old today.

According to *Cosmopolitan* magazine the most bankable stars in the cinema are Tom Cruise, Kevin Costner, Arnold Schwarzenegger and Mel Gibson.

Arnold Schwarzenegger

Monday May 25

Spring Bank Holiday

It's the hottest bank holiday since records began. Norwich hits 27°C (81°F). In Blackpool, a troupe of Russian ice dancers who arrive to rehearse their show, find the ice rink has melted into a puddle.

Tueday May 26

Residents of the Yorkshire village of Goathland, nr Whitby, which is the setting for the TV series *Heartbeat*, are worried about a tourist invasion this summer. There is only one public loo.

Wednesday May 27

The Swiss accidentally mobilize for war by pressing the wrong button and sending telegrams to the country's 3018 communes.

Littlehampton, Exmouth, Goodrington Sands, Sutton on Sea and Thorpe Bay are some of the 14 British beaches that have failed to meet EEC environmental and health standards.

Thursday May 28

Five desert tortoises, an endangered species, stop the construction of new homes in Hurrican, Utah, USA. If they stay, the houses will not be built.

Game wardens in Zimbabwe are starting to dehorn 300 black rhinos to try to save them from poachers.

Friday May 29

Eight runners from Bognor Regis, average age 61, arrive at Land's End after an 1414km relay from John O'Groats to raise money for cancer research.

The University of the Western Cape, S Africa, and a children's magazine, organize a children's forum to discuss the rights of children.

Saturday May 30

Helicopters drop tonnes of water on the Peak District National Park moorland fires. Smoke is visible for 112.6km.

Hoover and Beaver, two US Navy seals, are being retrained to film the feeding habits of whales.

Sunday May 31

A Hawker P1127, one of Britain's first jump jets, is dismantled and lifted through a third floor window to go on display at the Science Museum, South Kensington, London.

Ayrton Senna wins the Monaco Grand Prix.

Storms, flash floods and electricity cuts mark the end of the hot spell. It has been the hottest May for 150yrs.

1992

1 John & Norma Major
10 Downing Street

2 Margaret Becket
& John Smith

3

Left-right: Major, Princess of Wales, Callaghan, Prince of Wales, Wilson, the Queen, Heath, the Duke of Edinburgh & Thatcher

1 April 10
The Conservatives win the General Election with a majority of 21 seats

2 July 18
John Smith celebrates his election as leader of the Labour party

3 July 27
The Queen and the Duke of Edingburgh, together with the Prince and Princess of Wales, dine with five of her prime ministers to celebrate her 40th year on the throne

4 November 4
Bill Clinton becomes president of the USA, pictured here with Vice President Al Gore

1 April 12 Ex-hostage Terry Waite with the London Marathon winners Katrin Dorre & Antonio Pinto

2 May 9 Liverpool beats Sunderland 2-0 in the FA Cup final

3 July 4 Steffi Graff wins Wimbledon ladies' title

4 August 16 Nigel Mansell wins the world championship

5 November 14 England beats S Africa 33-16 in the 1st rugby international for 23yrs

June

Denmark wins the European Football Championship · Tower Bridge jams for the first time in 98 years

Monday June 1

█████████

🍦 Tenor Jose Carreras and soprano Sarah Brightman are to sing an anthem for the Olympic Games in Barcelona, *Friends for Life*, specially commissioned from Andrew Lloyd Webber and Don Black.

🍦 Cambridge bans all vehicles from the city centre.

Tuesday June 2

🍦 A referendum in Denmark rejects the Maastricht Treaty on a federal Europe.

🍦 A 15cm pin wheel falls an estimated 1828m from an aircraft narrowly missing Jimmy Rigby (45) of Stockport, Cheshire, standing in his garden.

Wednesday June 3

🍦 The Derby is won by *Dr Devious* ridden by John Reid.

🍦 150 nations take part in the UN Conference on the Environment and Development – the Earth Summit – which opens in Rio de Janiero, Brazil.

🍦 Judy Cross (48) of Foulden, Norfolk, is Postie of the Year. Her elderly customers hang a yellow duster in the window when they need shopping and help.

Thursday June 4

🍦 An Australian report published today says that Americans produce 863kg of rubbish per person per year. Australians produce 679kg each.

Friday June 5

🍦 Bird egg collectors are thought to have felled a 100yr old oak tree, where a pair of buzzards has been rearing young for 2yrs, at Llwydarth Farm in Maesteg, Mid Glam, to steal the eggs, worth £400 each.

🍦 Ex-prime minister Margaret Thatcher and 3 ex-chancellors become life peers in the Dissolution Honours.

Saturday June 6

🍦 Outgoing President Aquino of the Philippines is opening the presidential palace next week for free tours of Imelda Marcos's shoe collection (1220 pairs). Also on show will be her bullet-proof bra.

Sunday June 7

🍦 A bomb explodes outside the Festival Hall - no one is hurt.

🍦 The first part of *Diana: Her True Story* appears in *The Sunday Times* suggesting that the marriage of the Prince and Princess of Wales is over.

🍦 The Scott monument in Princes Street, Edinburgh, reopens after 2yrs closure.

Monday June 8

🍦 People in Britain drink 175 million cups of tea a day - more than 3 cups per day per person.

🍦 The Boxalls, a family of English settlers on Fetlar, Shetland Is. who answered a radio plea for more settlers *(see May 15)* find a hoard of Viking kitchenware while digging the garden. Archaeologists think their site is only the second Viking longhouse to be found in Shetland.

Tuesday June 9

🍦 Savvas Saritzoglu, a Greek hammer champion, carrying the torch bearing the Olympic flame on the first of stage of its journey from Greece to Barcelona, gives it to a man to hold while he has a rest. The man takes the torch and disappears. A new torch is on the way.

🍦 Salmon have returned to the River Trent after nearly a century.

Wednesday June 10

🍦 A woman shopping in Norwich hands over her watch, a gold tooth and a £50 cheque, before a wheel clamping firm allows her to drive her car away.

🍦 A replica of a 12th century Celtic galley, *Aileach*, sets sail from Loch Moidart on a 640km voyage to the Faroes and Shetland Is. using only sails and oars.

Thursday June 11

🍦 Captain Bill Pinkney (56) arrives back in Boston to become the first black American to sail solo round the world. He left Boston on August 5, 1990.

🍦 England draw 0-0 with Denmark in the opening European Football Championship match in Malmo, Sweden. Police break up riots.

Friday June 12

🍦 Sutton, Surrey, Council is offering wormeries of tiger worms to selected residents to try and save £2million a year on waste disposal costs. The worms will eat all the organic waste of a family of 4 except meat and fish scraps.

Saturday June 13

🍦 Astronaut Helen Sharman, cricketers Ian Botham and David Gower, and fashion designer Vivienne Westwood all receive OBEs, and comedian Spike Milligan receives an honorary CBE, in the Birthday honours.

Sunday June 14

🍦 Nigel Mansell fails to finish in the Canadian Grand Prix, which is won by Gerhard Berger.

🍦 The highest tower block of flats in Europe, built in the 1960s at Roystonhill, Glasgow, is blown up. Half a tonne of explosive stuffed into 5000 holes produces 20,000 tonnes of rubble.

Third night of rioting by English football supporters in Stockholm.

Monday June 15

The $35 million epic *Batman Returns* starring Michael Keaton, Michelle Pfeiffer as the Cat Woman and Danny de Vito as the Penguin, is a smash hit in the USA.

The House of Lords beats the House of Commons in the annual Tug o' War in aid of cancer relief.

Tuesday June 16

Germany beats Scotland 2-0 to force them out of the European Football Championsip at Norrkoping.

The Queen sends Paul McCartney a personal cheque towards the £13 million he is seeking to turn his old grammar school in Liverpool into an international school for the performing arts.

Wednesday June 17

Prince Edward opens the first two bays of the Globe Theatre on London's South Bank, which will allow scholars to make sure the right materials are used in the reconstruction.

London Zoo will close at the end of September because of lack of money.

England lose 2-1 to Sweden and are out of the European championship.

Stromness lifeboat rescues the crew of the replica 12th century longboat *Aileach* when it runs into difficulties in gale force winds NE of the Outer Hebrides.

Thursday June 18

625 acre Ramsey Island off the Welsh coast, home to 1 woman, 80,000 rabbits and a colony of grey seals, is for sale for £550,000.

The London Zoo Survival group, 240 staff members, look for ways to save the Zoo.

Friday June 19

National River Authority wardens are electro-stunning fish in the Hole Brook, a tributary of the R Okemont, Devon, and taking them to safety, after 45,000 litres of farm slurry pours into it.

Michael Jackson is bringing 2 tonnes of costumes to Europe for his *Dangerous* tour.

Saturday June 20

Planet Hollywood, the restaurant owned by Sylvester Stallone, Bruce Willis and Arnold Schwarzenegger, is to open in London.

US sporting superstar Carl Lewis fails to qualify to represent the USA in the 100m at the Olympic Games in Barcelona despite being the world record holder over the distance (9.86secs) and already the winner of 12 Olympic medals.

Sunday June 21

More than 27,000 cyclists take part in the annual London - Brighton cycle ride in aid of the British Heart Foundation.

The Prince and Princess of Wales open part of the grounds of Highgrove to the public for the first time.

Monday June 22

The beginning of the Wimbledon championships.

An anonymous buyer pays £4,620 for a 12.7cm lock of Byron's hair as a present for his son, a student at Cambridge.

Tuesday June 23

The Emir of Kuwait donates £1 million to help save London Zoo.

Work stops at the Guildhall, London, on the site of a planned art gallery, because a pair of rare black redstarts have built a nest. The developers must wait until the eggs hatch in August.

Wednesday June 24

Artists from 5 European nations will be part of the Olympic teams this year to record events as they happen. Britain's representative is photo-artist David Hiscock (35).

A letter from the composer Mozart to his wife Constanza sells for £60,500 at Christie's, London.

Thursday June 25

The government gives the go ahead for the £25 million Skye bridge to be built.

The *Columbia* space shuttle blasts off on a 13 day mission. The 7 astronauts will light small controlled fires and grow protein and mineral crystals.

Friday June 26

Denmark beat Germany 2-0 in Gothenburg to win the European Football Championship.

Aileach, the 12th century longboat, which set off from Loch Moidart on June 10, reaches the Faroe Is.

Saturday June 27

An Australian/Russian rescue team finds 32 scientists who have lived for 4 months on a floating ice flow off Antarctica.

Sunday June 28

National Music Day

California, USA, suffers the worst earthquake for 40yrs measuring 7.4 on the Richter scale.

A new fungus, forty times bigger than the one in Michigan *(see April 1)*, has been found in Washington State, USA.

Monday June 29

Farmers and landowners in the Cambridgeshire fens are being offered poplar trees to plant to help save the rare golden oriel. Only 30 pairs breed in Britain, and the birds are under threat because not enough poplars are growing to replace mature trees.

Tuesday June 30

- the 2nd this month

Tower Bridge jams for the first time, 98yrs to the day since it first opened.

The Girl Guide Association drops the word 'girl' from the title to appeal to teenagers.

It's been the warmest June since records began in 1659.

July

Britain takes on EEC presidency for 6 months · Lady Helen Windsor marries · Opening of Barcelona Olympic Games

Wednesday July 1

A 11.3m high totem pole carved by Norman Tart - an American Indian chief - is raised in Bushey Park to mark Canada Day.

Thursday July 2

Islamic new year (1413)

St Tiggywinkles Hospital in Aylesbury is treating more than 1000 animals suffering from dehydration and malnutrition because of the drought. Badgers are the worst hit.

At the International Whaling Commission conference in Glasgow, Britain blocks an attempt to lift the ban on commercial whaling; it will run for one more year.

Friday July 3

No play at Wimbledon because of rain. For the first time the unhappy tennis fans will get a full refund or tickets for the same day next year.

Saturday July 4

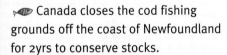

Steffi Graff wins the Wimbledon ladies' title beating Monica Seles 6-2, 6-1 in 5½hrs of which only 58mins is spent on court because of rain.

Canada closes the cod fishing grounds off the coast of Newfoundland for 2yrs to conserve stocks.

Sunday July 5

Andre Agassi wins the men's singles title at Wimbledon beating Goran Ivanisevic 6-7, 6-4, 6-4, 1-6, 6-4 in 2hrs 50mins.

Nigel Mansell wins the French Grand Prix at Magny Cours, his sixth victory this year. He now equals Jackie Stewart's record 27 grand prix wins.

David Gower becomes the highest scoring batsman in English test history beating Geoff Boycott's 8,114 runs with his 73 against Pakistan at Old Trafford.

Monday July 6

Network Southeast are installing black box recorders in all their trains to improve passenger safety.

Tuesday July 7

Salvage experts discover that hundreds of bottles of whisky have been stolen from the wreck of a Swedish ship in the North Sea of Skinningrove, Cleveland.

Footballer Paul Gascoigne arrives in Rome to start his career with Lazio.

Wednesday July 8

A BA flight from London to Newcastle gets two RAF Tornadoes as an escort to celebrate being the 5 millionth customer of the RAF's Eastern Radar Unit (part of the National Air Traffic service).

Thursday July 9

An illegally dumped oil slick slithers along the coast towards Redcar, Yorks, and threatens the breeding ground of the rare little terns.

Daley Thompson (33) Britain's record-breaking decathlete, retires from athletics.

The space shuttle *Columbia* arrives back in Florida after a 14 day research programme and the longest shuttle flight.

Friday July 10

Children in the Bradford area have been asked to collect 2 billion daisy leaves by researchers at Bradford Royal Infirmary to help in a new treatment for Aids. Monday is Daisy Day, when children are asked to deliver their daisy leaves.

Saturday July 11

An American boy (11) is attempting to divorce his mother and father in court, in Florida, on the grounds that he has been neglected and abandoned. He wants to be adopted by the foster parents he has lived with for 9 months.

Sunday July 12

Nigel Mansell wins the British Grand Prix at Silverstone and leads the World Championship by 36 points: it's his 7th win this year and 28th overall.

Luke McShane (8) of Chelsea, London, becomes the youngest chess master in the history of the game by winning the World Under 10 championship in Duisberg, Germany, losing only 1 game out of 11.

Monday July 13

Ganesh Sittampelam (13) mathematics prodigy of Surbiton, a pupil at King's College Junior School, Wimbledon, has become Britain's youngest first class honours graduate. He covered the first year of the degree course before he enrolled, and completed the rest in 60 days going 1 day a week to Surrey University.

Tuesday July 14

A primitive iron golf club forged by an 18th century Scottish blacksmith is sold for £92,400 at Sothebys.

Tower Bridge is in action 11 times today to let through a French destroyer, a cruise liner, ocean going tugs and sailing barges as well as tourist and commercial traffic. It usually opens about 10 times a week.

Wednesday July 15

St Swithin's Day

A bomb disposal team blows up two packets left outside an army depot in Totnes, Devon, to find they contain frozen chips.

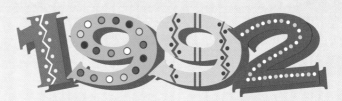

1992 Olympic Games

February 8th, Winter Olympics open in Albertville, France
July 25th, Olympic Games open in Barcelona, Spain
Bringing home the medals...

1 July 25 Steve Redgrave carries the flag for Britain

2 August 2 Steve Redgrave & Matthew Pinsent (GB) - *pictured here* - win gold in the Coxless Pairs and Greg & Jonathan Searle (GB) win gold in the Coxed Pairs

3 August 1 Linford Christie (GB) wins the 100m – the oldest man ever to win

4 July 29 Chris Boardman (GB) wins the gold medal in the Individual 4000m Cycling event

5 August 3 Simon Terry (GB) wins the bronze medal in the 70m Archery

6 August 4 Sally Gunnell (GB) wins the gold medal in the 400m Hurdles

7 August 6 Kriss Akabusi (GB) wins the bronze medal in the 400m Hurdles

Olympic Medal Table *(Top Three)*

		G	S	B	Total
1	Unified Team (12 former republics)	45	38	29	112
2	USA	37	34	37	108
3	Germany	37	21	28	82
12	Great Britain	5	3	12	20

More than 150 Australian volunteers working in freezing weather rescue 44 beached whales at Seal Rock, NSW, Australia.

Thursday July 16

A glow-in-the-dark lavatory seat designed by Clint Lenz (10) from Lake Mills, Wisconsin, USA, wins the household division prize in a national inventions competition. It will go on show at the Smithsonian Institution, Washington.

Friday July 17

Farmer John Liddiard (56) of Great Shefford, Berks, has to remove two lifesize cardboard scarecrows of men with guns, because the local rights-of-way officer thinks they will frighten picnickers and ramblers.

Saturday July 18

John Smith is elected leader of the Labour party.

Lady Helen Windsor marries Tim Taylor at St George's Chapel, Windsor.

Rainbow trout, elephant fish and golden orfe compete for the job of water monitor of toxic levels at Thames Water's treatment works on the R Tillingbourne in Surrey.

Sunday July 19

Nick Faldo wins his third Open golf championship at Muirfield.

The Walt Disney organization has applied to be allowed to take over the US naval base at Subic Bay in the Philippines to make it another Disneyland.

Monday July 20

Scientists at Leicester University have discovered what may be the hottest star in our galaxy with a temperature 70°C higher than the sun and 1700 times hotter than boiling water.

Tuesday July 21

£110,000, the world record price for a racing pigeon, is paid for a 4yr-old bird which was flown into Gatwick from Amsterdam and taken to its new home in a Rolls Royce.

English artist and writer John Bratby (64) dies.

Wednesday July 22

Two thirds of the French people want Marie Curie, who discovered radium, to be the first woman to be buried in the Pantheon national memorial in Paris.

Thursday July 23

After a 2 hour struggle, two fisherman land a 5 tonne shark off the Durham coast when it becomes entangled in their nets and tows their boat, the *Lady Lydia*, out to sea.

Friday July 24

The 25th Olympic Games are opened in Barcelona by King Juan Carlos. 172 countries are taking part, and for the first time in 32 years the games are not troubled by political disputes.

Saturday July 25

23,000 people attend the first Sunday race meeting to be held in Britain at Doncaster.

Guy Haslam (29), editor of *The Puzzler* magazine, becomes the youngest winner of *The Times* Intercity Crossword Championship completing four puzzles in the average time of $9\frac{1}{2}$ mins per puzzle.

Miguel Indurain wins the Tour de France for the second year running.

Sunday July 26

Keb Soon Yeo (18) of S Korea wins the first gold medal of the 1992 Olympic Games for the 10 Metre Rifle Competition.

Nigel Mansell wins the German Grand Prix at Hockenheim.

Monday July 27

The Shell Junior Mileage Marathon is won by Belfairs High School, Leigh on Sea, Essex, with a car that does 536kpl.

Five prime ministers, Major, Thatcher, Callaghan, Wilson and Heath give a dinner at 10 Downing Street for the Queen and the Duke of Edinburgh to celebrate the 40th anniversary of the Queen's reign.

Tuesday July 28

Dame Jocelyn Barrow, deputy chairman of the Broadcasting Standards Council and the first black woman living in Great Britian to be awarded the title, receives her honour from the Queen.

Mingxia Fu (13) from China, becomes the youngest Olympic diving champion when she wins the gold medal at the Barcelona Olympics by a massive 50 points.

Wednesday July 29

E Anglia is invaded by hundreds of thousands of butterflies crossing the North Sea, particulary Large Whites, which are threatening the Suffolk cabbage crop.

Chris Boardman, on his revolutionary Lotus bicycle, wins Britain's first Olympic gold medal in the Individual 400m Cycling event.

Thursday July 30

Footballer Gary Lineker arrives in Nagoya, Japan, to meet the managers and players of Grampus, the club he will join for 2yrs in February. He is already learning Japanese.

SAS troops are guarding the nests of peregrine falcons at Kielder Forest, Northumberland. Thousands of young birds worth more than £1000 each are stolen each year.

Friday July 31

The remains of the 18thC Danish navigator Vitus Bering, who gave his name to the Bering Straits and died in a shipwreck in 1741, have been found on an island off Russia's Kamchatka Peninsula. They will be formally buried in September.

World War II hero and founder of the Cheshire homes, Group Captain Leonard Cheshire, dies aged 74.

August

Saturday August 1

Linford Christie (GB) wins the 100m at the Barcelona Olympics in a time of 9.96secs, at 32yrs the oldest man ever to win the 100m.

Swimmer Matt Biondi (USA) wins 11 medals (8 gold, 2 silver and 1 bronze) to equal the record of Mark Spitz (USA) in the Olympic pool.

Sunday August 2

Star Safaris, a tour of the homes and clubs of the rich and famous, is launched in London. Included in the tour are the homes of Jason Donovan, Michael Heseltine, Andrew Lloyd Webber, Joan Collins, Tina Tuner, and Freddie Mercury.

Amy Kleinhaus (24) of Cape Town, becomes the first coloured woman to be chosen Miss South Africa.

Monday August 3

Simon Terry (GB) takes Britain's first individual Olympic medal in archery since 1908 when he wins the bronze medal in the 70m.

As an experiment, two apartments in Hampton Court Palace are to be let to holidaymakers.

Tuesday August 4

National Plain English Day - dedicated to getting rid off gobbledygook.

Sally Gunnell (26) becomes the first British woman to win an Olympic track event since 1964 when she takes the gold medal in the 400m hurdles.

Mars bars celebrate their 60th birthday.

Wednesday August 5

A Dutch scientific organization has designed a car that corrects bad driving. It will lift pressure on the accelerator if the driver is driving too fast or too close to the car in front.

A tiny electronic bug that is small enough to fit into woodworm holes has been developed and may finally defeat thieves of antiques and pictures.

Thursday August 6

Kriss Akabusi (GB), who is retiring from athletics after the Olympic Games, wins a bronze medal in the 400m hurdles setting a national record. Carl Lewis (USA) retains his long jump title and gains his seventh Olympic gold medal.

Friday August 7

Andrew Moffatt, a Lothian Region water worker discovers pieces of pottery, a necklace and human teeth in a dried up part of a reservoir nr Whinton in the borders. It is the site of seven bronze age graves.

The QE II runs aground on a sandbank off Massachusetts, USA

Saturday August 8

Scott Killen (36) from Montreal, gets himself into the *Guinness Book of Records* by shaking the hands of 25,289 people in 8hrs at the Canadian pavilion at Expo 92 in Seville, Spain.

Sunday August 9

The spectacular closing ceremony of the Olympic Games in Barcelona is watched on television by an estimated worldwide audience of 2 billion.

An Italian powerboat wins the Virgin Atlantic Challenge Trophy by crossing the Atlantic in 58hrs 34mins 4secs, knocking 21hrs of the previous record.

Monday August 10

The QE11 limps into Boston dry dock for repairs.

After 40yrs service at Severn Trent Water, Michael Coates is offered the choice of a holiday in the Seychelles, or a season ticket to Sheffield United FC until the next century. Sheffield United wins.

Tuesday August 11

Mexico's minister of sport, Raul Gonzalez, resigns because of Mexico's miserable showing in the Olympics; they won just one medal - silver - in the 50km walk.

Mount Pinatubo volcano in the Philippines erupts for the second time in 14 months. 70,000 people may have to be evacuated.

Wednesday August 12

The start of the year's most spectacular heavenly light show - look out for the Perseid Meteor shower, which could be the most dramatic this century.

A new ferry service threatens the worlds shortest scheduled air flight - 2 mins between Westray and Papa Westray in the Orkney Islands - Loganair has been running the service for 25yrs.

Thursday August 13

International Left-Handers Day. Covent Garden celebrates with everything for the left-hander from books that open the wrong way to left-handed boomerangs. *(Famous left-handers are Prince William, Picasso, Einstein, Leonardo da Vinci, Marilyn Monroe.)*

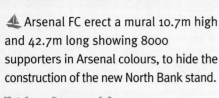

Arsenal FC erect a mural 10.7m high and 42.7m long showing 8000 supporters in Arsenal colours, to hide the construction of the new North Bank stand.

Friday August 14

Thousands of fans buy a set of 9 Elvis Presley stamps issued by St Vincent and Grenadines to mark the 15th anniversary of the singer's death.

The Coca Cola Corporation in Italy apologizes to Greece for running an advertisement showing the Parthenon columns tapered like cola bottles.

Saturday August 15

Start of a series of 40 matches between Dr Marion Tinsley, the Draughts World Champion for 38yrs, and a Canadian computer called Chinook at the Park Lane Hotel, London.

Sunday August 16

National Peat Bog Day. Peat bogs are open to the public.

Nigel Mansell comes in second at the Hungarian Grand Prix, and wins the World Formula 1 championship. He has been runner up three times.

Greenland launches an official Santa Claus post office.

Monday August 17

Essex fire brigade say that swarms of thunderflies are setting off fire alarms, which mistake them for smoke.

Mount Everest is so popular with climbers, who leave their litter behind them, that all climbing teams must now deposit £2000 towards rubbish removal.

Tuesday August 18

Harry Schuler (24), a NZ electrician who can scream louder than hi-fi stereo systems, breaks the world screaming record in Christchurch, NZ, with a scream measured at 130 decibels.

Draughts champion Dr Marion Tinsley has taken the lead against the Chinook computer (see Aug 15).

Wednesday August 19

Rock art more than 40,000 years old has been found in th Olary region of S Australia.

The Chinook computer draws level with draughts champion Dr Marion Tinsley at 7 games all (see Aug 15).

Thursday August 20

A pair of peregrine falcons is rearing their young 91.5m up the tower of Liverpool's Anglican cathedral.

Chinook the computer takes the lead in the draughts match against the world champion Dr Marion Tinsley.

Friday August 21

Heavy rain triggers a river of steaming mud from Mount Pinatubo in the Philippines. Nearly 250,000 people flee the area.

Forest fires reduce the town of Round Mount, California, to ruins and force 14,000 people from their homes.

Saturday August 22

Chinook the computer breaks down at 10 games all in its match against world draughts champion Dr Marion Tinsley.

Wild fires rampage across Utah, Oregon, California and Idaho, USA.

Sunday August 23

Hurricane Andrew hits the Florida coast with gusts up to 217kph. Nearly 1 million people are evacuated.

A 17thC Florentine casket worth £200,000 is stolen from the Victoria & Albert museum during opening hours.

Monday August 24

World draughts champion Dr Marion Tinsley, now leads Chinook by 3 to 2 with 21 draws.

Giant Japanese whelks, ten times the size of the British ones, have been found on the Dogger Bank in the N Sea.

Tuesday August 25

Thousands flee New Orleans as Hurricane Andrew screams across the Gulf of Mexico.

Edward Webb (20) the great great nephew of Capt Matthew Webb, the first man to swim the Channel, has to turn back just 804m from Dover in his attempt to parascend across.

Wednesday August 26

John Lennon's draft for A Day in the Life sells for £48,400 and Paul McCartney's She's Leaving Home fetches £45,100 in a sale at Sotheby's.

Thursday August 27

The filming of Jurassic Park, Steven Spielberg's film about genetically engineered dinosaurs, begins on Hauai Island's north shore, Hawaii.

Hurricane Andrew whips into Louisiana. It is the costliest natural disaster in American history.

Friday August 28

A Los Angeles, USA, writer produces a book called Literary Licences which retells well-known stories using nothing but a selection of the million or so personalized licence plates in the greater Los Angeles area.

Saturday August 29

World draughts champion Dr Marion Tinsley gains a crushing victory over Chinook in the 39th game with a 2 game lead (see Aug 15).

Hong Kong samples the delights of fish and chips with the opening of the first Harry Ramsden shop.

Mary Norton, author of The Borrowers series, dies aged 88.

Sunday August 30

Rain almost washes out the Notting Hill carnival, London, for the first time in 6yrs.

Stewart Paton and Simon Stephenson of Lymington, Hants, complete an 8 week walk on stilts from Lands End to John o' Groats.

Monday August 31

Bank holiday

The three-day Reading Pop Festival ends in a sea of mud.

Wind and rain lash deserted beaches. It's been the wettest August for 4yrs.

Farmers on New Zealand's South Island are digging out thousands of sheep in the worst snow storm they've had for 30yrs.

September

Tuesday September 1

✎ Longleat welcomes its 20 millionth visitor in its 40th anniversary year.

✎ Farmers at Minchinhampton, Glos, have fitted flourescent collars to their cows as so many have been injured by cars at night.

✎ In the USA, 250,000 people have been made homeless by Hurricane Andrew.

Wednesday September 2

✎ Singer Gloria Estefan and a group of volunteers have turned her Miami offices into a distrubution centre for nappies, food and water, for those made homeless by Hurricane Andrew.

✎ An undersea earthquake sends 9.15m high tidal waves crashing onto the shore along a 290km stretch of coast in Nicaragua.

Thursday September 3

✎ Pop star Prince (also known as The Purple One, His Purpleness and the Prince of Weird) signs a recording deal with Warner Brothers worth $54 million and giving him an executive role as Vice President. He also gets $60 million for 6 albums over the next 6yrs, and $48 million for *Paisley Park*, his own record label.

Friday September 4

✎ The United Nations appoints a special envoy in Kenya to lead attempts to preserve rhinos from extinction.

✎ Two Belgians flying across Europe in a motorised hang glider to celebrate the end of the Cold War are arrested in the Ukraine for flying over a military airport.

Saturday September 5

✎ Six million people have visited Euro Disney since it opened on April 12.

✎ Mike Oldfield's *Tubular Bells II*, released last week has sold more than 300,000 copies, 20yrs after his first *Tubular Bells* appeared.

Sunday September 6

✎ Don Wales (21) grandson of speed ace Sir Malcolm Campbell, is going to try and beat the world land speed record for electric cars in Bluebird 9. The record is currently held by Roger Hedlund (US) .

Monday September 7

✎ Classic FM , the first national commercial competitor for the BBC in 70yrs, begins broadcasting.

✎ The French saleroom Druot sells 121 lots of old jeans, including two 1930's Big E Jeans. A cardboard cutout of cowboy Gene Autry wearing the original 501s sells for 130,000Fr.

Tuesday September 8

✎ President Bush asks Congress for £3.8 billion to rebuild the damage caused by Hurricane Andrew.

✎ Katherine Brown (17) from Tiffin Girls School, Kingston, becomes the first woman to win a place in the schools' finals of the Toshiba Invention of the Year, with her electronic fencing partner.

Wednesday September 9

✎ School starts at 8.30am with just 30mins for lunch for pupils at four schools on Merseyside to allow them to finish school at 2pm and give them a chance to do their homework before watching the evening soaps.

Thursday September 10

✎ The transmitters that used to jam the BBC World Service broadcasts to the former Soviet Union have been hired by the World Service to beam Mandarin and English programmes into China.

Friday September 11

✎ For the first time, no polio cases have been reported in the Americas for one year. Experts ask the WHO to certify that the disease is eliminated from the Western hemisphere.

Saturday September 12

✎ US prepares to make the most expensive (£84,000) loaf ever baked as astronauts on the space shuttle *Endeavour* try to make a small loaf to see if yeast will make dough rise in near zero gravity.

✎ 300 people attend the first Archers convention in Birmingham.

✎ Film star Anthony Perkins, best remembered for his role in *Psycho*, dies aged 60.

Sunday September 13

✎ Nigel Mansell (39) announces his retirement from Formula 1 motor racing.

✎ Edward Webb, the great great nephew of the first man to swim the Channel, crosses from Dover to Calais on his fourth attempt, harnessed to a parachute.

✎ President Bush declares much of the Pacific a disaster area just an hour after Hawaii is hit by Hurricane Iniki on Friday night with wind gusts up to 160kph.

Monday September 14

✎ The foundations of the new Severn Road Bridge, 5km downstream from the present bridge, are unveiled.

✎ Nigel Mansell, who has failed to reach agreement on terms to continue with the Williams racing team, is considering joining the Newman-Haas Indy car racing team.

1992

TOP TEN FILMS

1. **Basic Instinct**
2. **Hook**
3. **Lethal Weapon III**
4. **Batman Returns**
5. **Cape Fear**
6. **Beauty and the Beast**
7. **Wayne's World**
8. **Home Alone 2: Lost in New York**
9. **My Girl**
10. **The Hand that Rocks the Cradle**

Left & Below: Robin Williams & Dustin Hoffman star in Hook

Lethal Weapon III

Michelle Pfeiffer as Cat Woman

Michael Keaton as Batman

Beauty and the Beast

Basic Instinct

Waynes World

Left: Macaulay Culkin in Home Alone 2

The Hand that Rocks the Cradle

Left & below: Anna Chlumsky & Macaulay Culkin in My Girl

Tuesday September 15

🖊 A bag of bones, believed to include the remains of the murdered Russian royal family, arrives by air for forensic examination in Britain.

Wednesday September 16

🖊 Black Wednesday: After an expensive fight to defend the £, Britain suspends its membership of ERM to allow sterling to float.

Thursday September 17

🖊 Forensic scientists start testing the bones which may hold the secret of what happened to Tsar Nicholas II and his family. A sample of hair from the Duke of Edinburgh, whose grandmother was a sister of the tsarina, may help identify the DNA sequence *(see Sept 15)*.

Friday September 18

🖊 The Grandparent of the Year award sponsored by Cadbury and Age Concern goes to Mary Edwards (69) of Prestatyn, Clwyd.

🖊 Nigel Mansell signs with the Newman Haas Indy car racing team for a fee of £3 million.

🖊 Thunderstorms and torrential rain flood villages in Somerset and Wiltshire. Lightning strikes the tower of Norwich Cathedral.

Saturday September 19

🖊 Susan Moon (12) of Crowthorne, Berks, becomes Choir Girl of the Year.

🖊 The last RAF Vulcan bomber makes its final flight at Cranfield, Beds.

🖊 Famous Welsh baritone Sir Geraint Evans (70) dies.

Sunday September 20

🖊 At the biggest ever enactment of a civil war battle, to mark the 350th anniversary of the 1642 Battle of Powick Bridge, Worcs, nineteen people are hurt.

🖊 Robert Holland of Cumnock, Strathclyde, shows the world's biggest onion (5.07kg) at the National Kelsae Onion Festival in Harrogate, N. Yorks.

Monday September 21

🖊 The first Transatlantic Balloon Race, which left Bangor, Maine, USA, last Wednesday, is won by the Belgian team who covered the 4151km in 115 hours. British balloonists Don Cameron and Rob Bayley, who land on the coast of Portugal are second, 8hrs behind the winners.

Tuesday September 22

🖊 British postmen get a new bike - the first new design in 60 years - provided they cycle more than 4827km a year.

🖊 Tony Bradley and Richard Arbruzzo (US) land nr Casablanca, Morocco after 146hrs - the longest flight by a hot air balloon - and come third in the Transatlantic Balloon Race.

Wednesday September 23

🖊 British Aerospace announce the closure of their Hatfield factory where such famous planes as the *Tiger Moth*, the *Mosquito* bomber and the *Comet*, the world's first jet plane, were produced.

🖊 E England flooded as a month's rain falls in a few hours.

🖊 Paul Gascoigne plays for Lazio against his old team Tottenham Hotspur in Rome. He scores the first goal, and creates the second in Lazio's 3-0 win.

Thursday September 24

🖊 Phil Stevens (24), a milkman, follows a gang of thieves in his 32kph milk float when he hears a burglar alarm on his delivery round in Shepton Mallet, Som. A man is later arrested.

Friday September 25

🖊 Gregory Kingsley (12) wins a landmark children's rights case in Florida when he is allowed to divorce his parents and be adopted by his foster family. *(see July 11)*

Saturday September 26

🖊 ~~██████~~ 🌙

🖊 Start of Chay Blythe's British Steel Challenge Round the World race against the prevailing winds. A 10 strong fleet of identical boats, 20m long steel yachts, sets off at 12 noon.

Sunday September 27

🖊 Neil Kinnock, ex-leader of the Labour Party, will take over the Jimmy Young Show on Radio One for one week in November.

🖊 Lady Beaumont of Birley Gate, nr. Hereford, has bred the smallest donkey in Britain. It is an American Sicilian donkey, is 50cm high, and is unlikely to get any bigger than 75cm.

Monday September 28

🖊 Jewish new year (5755)

🖊 Big Breakfast goes on air on Channel 4.

Tuesday September 29

🖊 David Appleby, a pet behaviour counsellor, has treatred more than 100 pets at the RSPCA's psychology clinic in Leicester, including one dog who slept on its owners' bed, but bit them every time they turned over.

Wednesday September 30

🖊 It's the 25th anniversary of Radio One. Alan Freeman *(right)* and John Peel *(below right)* are the only survivors from the original line up of DJs.

🖊 The new 10p coin is launched.

🖊 Leeds United beat Stuttgart by 4-1, but are out of the European Cup on away goals.

October

Giant beetroot claims world record • New Planet 1992 QB1 discovered beyond Pluto • Thousands march in support of miners

Thursday October 1

Scientists at the Scottish Agricultural College, Edinburgh, have produced a football food dispenser for pigs that dispenses food as it rolls around. It teaches the pigs to root for morsels of food as they would in the wild.

Friday October 2

Singer Dame Kiri te Kanawa is artist of the year, and conductor Sir Georg Solti wins the lifetime achievement award at the Gramaphone Awards ceremony at the Dorchester Hotel, London.

Police are called to sheltered housing in Uttoxeter when the noise from a pensioners' karaoke night gets out of hand.

Saturday October 3

An El-Al cargo jet plunges into two blocks of flats in Amsterdam minutes after taking off. 150-200 people are feared dead.

Akio Monta, head of Sony and the man who gave the world the Walkman, receives an honorary knighthood from the Queen.

Sunday October 4

Parrots worth £25,000 are stolen from Paradise Park, Hayle, Cornwall. The birds are fitted with electronic implants which can be matched against a register of rare birds, which will make them difficult to sell.

A giant beetroot weighing 17.12kg on show at the Giant Vegetable Competition at Newport, Gwent, claims the world record.

A tornado with winds gusting up to 145kph hits Florida.

Monday October 5

Sylvester Stallone pays £13,500 for a Tardis said to have been used by William Hartnell, the first Dr Who, in the BBC series that featured the Daleks.

It is the 50th birthday of Oxfam.

Tuesday October 6

Astronomers at the University of Hawaii discover a new planet beyond Pluto and so far called 1992 QB1. Reddish in colour, dark, with eternal permafrost, it is only 200km across, and revolves round the sun once every 262yrs. It is the most distant object in the solar system yet identified by man.

Wedensday October 7

Chocolate-flavoured potato crisps, produced by the people who first brought you spring onion and tomato flavoured crisps, are being tested in NE England and Scotland.

Thursday October 8

Rabbit ears worn by Dr Spock in *Star Trek* and donated by Leonard Nimoy, raise £700 in Christie's Charity Auction for the London Federation of Boys' Clubs.

Friday October 9

The *Pioneer* spacecraft plunges into the scorching atmosphere of Venus ending its 14yr mission. Launched in 1978 to study Venus, the fuel ran out earlier this week.

A whale, in a Japanese aquarium, has given birth to a baby fathered by a bottle-nose dolphin. The 'Whalephin' was about 1.8m long when born.

Saturday October 10

The hole in the ozone layer over the Antarctic now extends to cover the tip of S America and the Falkland Is.

Conservation International report that a pocket-sized monkey with a koala-like face and named the Maues Marmoset, has been discovered in a remote part of the Amazon.

Sunday October 11

Cambridge beats Oxford by 1/10th of a point to lead the table of top universities, followed by Imperial College, London and Edinburgh.

A goat that fell off the cliffs on Lundy Is in the Bristol Channel has swum to a tiny island nearby. The 36.6m rocky outcrop will probably feed it, but it may not be able to withstand the winter gales.

Monday October 12

NASA launches a 2yr $100 million programme to search for aliens.

England draw 1-1 with Norway in the opening game of the World Cup qualifying match at Wembley. David Platt is the goal scorer.

Tuesday October 13

An earthquake in Cairo, Egypt, measuring 5.8 on the Richter scale and lasting one minute, kills 370 and injures 3369.

British Coal announces that it is to close 31 pits with the loss of 31,000 jobs.

Wednesday October 14

Laure Hsiao Sun, a Chinese-American woman, pays £100,000 at China's first international auction in Peking for a black limousine said to belong to Chairman Mao.

Thursday October 15

Police install 21 cameras at accident black spots around London to check speeding motorists.

Three Belgian art students have done such a good job painting graffitti on lavatory walls that the city council of Ghent has asked them to paint all 50 of their public loos.

🎃 Heavy snow in Glenshee.

Friday October 16

🎃 The EEC conference opens in Birmingham.

🎃 Singer Bob Dylan is joined by ex-Beatle George Harrison at his 30th anniversary concert in New York.

🎃 Stephen Hendry is voted *Snooker Player of the Year*, and Peter Ebdon *Newcomer of the Year* in the World Professional Billiards & Snooker Association's annual awards.

Saturday October 17

🎃 The crew of a Russian ship at Immingham, Humberside, refuse to leave until customs officers return their monkey. Customs say it is an endangered species and must go to a zoo.

Sunday October 18

🎃 Thousands of people march in support of the miners and against the closure of 31 pits.

🎃 Hungary's famous white Lippizaner horses are under threat. They are too slow for racing, and too plump to jump, and have until now been subsidized by the government.

Monday October 19

🎃 The Queen and Duke of Edinburgh arrive in Germany at the start of their state visit.

🎃 Despite the agreement signed in Madrid last year, Britain wants to keep its 20 huskies in the Antarctic until they die of old age, as it is the only home they have known. Huskies have been there since 1945.

Tuesday October 20

🎃 Kate Bishop (15) of Hythe, Kent, wins Sainsbury's Future Cook award at the Savoy Hotel, London, beating 7 other finalists and 30,000 entrants aged 12-15.

Wednesday October 21

🎃 Hundreds of thousands of people form a 5km long column on a march around Hyde Park in support of the miners and against the proposed pit closures.

Thursday October 22

🎃 Among the participants at the Scottish Storytelling Festival at the Royal Botanic Gardens, Edinburgh, is Red Thundercloud - the last native speaker of the American *Catawba* tribe. He is also an expert in making herbal teas, and conducts herbal walks around the gardens.

Friday October 23

🎃 National Woggle Day.

🎃 Charles Cockell, an Oxford researcher, reveals his plan to trek 644km across the southern pole of Mars. He hopes to convince NASA, to support him.

Saturday October 24

🎃 Summertime ends. Clocks go back at 2am.

🎃 The Dyfed Wildlife Trust wants 100 companies each to pay £300 to adopt one of the bottle-nosed dolphins in Cardigan Bay.

Sunday October 25

🎃

🎃 50th anniversary of the Battle of El Alamein.

🎃 Goldie (14), the Blue Peter dog, dies. She made 650 appearances on the programme 1978-1986 *(see below)*.

🎃 Nigel Mansell pulls over and lets his teammate Riccardo Patrese win the

Japanese Grand Prix to take 2nd place in the World Driver's championship

Monday October 26

🎃 Grand pageant at Earls Court to celebrate the 40th anniversary of the Queen's reign.

🎃 Jordy Lemone (4), has been top of the pop charts in France for the past two weeks with his song *Dur dur d'etre Bebe (It's Hard to be a Baby)*.

Tuesday October 27

🎃 Richard Gabriel (38) a former motor-cycle dispatch rider, who started a dispatch company and sold it for £50 million, is voted Britain's most romantic top tycoon. He was nominated by his secretary.

Wednesday October 28

🎃 Sixty high-speed trains a day will run between London, Paris and Brussels when the international rail

service, to be called Eurostar, is launched in the summer of 1994. The journey time between London and Paris will be 3hrs.

Thursday October 29

🎃 A 498.3kg female sturgeon, possibly the biggest fish ever caught, is netted in the Yangtse River, China. Scientists who land the fish think it might be 100yrs old.

Friday October 30

🎃 A car bomb explodes nr Downing Street, when a minicab driver is hijacked and forced at gunpoint to drive to Whitehall.

🎃 Six members of a Sino-Japanese expedition climb the world's highest unconquered peak Namcha Barwa (7,787m) Tibet.

Saturday October 31

🎃 Hallowe'en

🎃 The Army Air Corps transports 200 tonnes of stone to Dunkery Beacon on Exmoor to repair erosion caused by tourists.

1992
Annus Horribilis

November 24 Queen describes 1992 as her 'annus horribilis' at the 40th anniversary lunch given by the Lord Mayor of London

Prince Andrew

Fergie & Beatrice

Prince Charles

March 20 Buckingham Palace announces the separation of the Duke and Duchess of York

December 9 Buckingham Palace announces the separation of the Prince and Princess of Wales

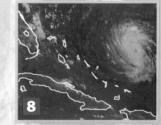

DAILY Mirror
INSIDE 12 PAGE ROYAL SOUVENIR
No kids and no husband – back to an empty house
HOME ALONE
TURN TO PAGES 2,3,4,5,6,7,9,24 and 25

Princess Diana

November 20
1 Windsor Castle on fire
2 Firemen tackling the blaze
3 State apartments wrecked
4 The Queen talks with firemen

Other Disasters...

5 April 10 The Baltic Exchange, London, showing the damage caused by the IRA bomb

6 April 10 Helping the injured at the Baltic Exchange

7 April 14 Lava from Mt Etna almost engulfs a house at Zafferana, Sicily

8 August 22 Satellite photo of Hurricane Andrew heading towards the Miami coast

9 October 4 El Al Cargo Boeing crashes into an apartment block in Amsterdam, Holland

November

70th Anniversary of broadcasting by BBC • Fire sweeps Windsor Castle • Queen calls 1992 her 'annus horribilis'

Sunday November 1

☂ 400 vehicles take part in the London to Brighton Veteran Car Run and manage the 96.5km in 3hrs 10mins. The first to finish is Dennis Nicholls in his 1899 Romain tricycle.

☂ A Boeing 747 from Istanbul loses an engine when it lands in thick fog in Luxembourg. The engine is found 90m from the plane.

Monday November 2

☂ Channel 4 is 10yrs old.

☂ Eight men and women, half way through the 2yr long Biosphere experiment in the Arizona Desert, are suffering from loss of oxygen. 15-30% of the 3,800 species of plants in the biosphere have died, and the bees and hummingbirds have disappeared.

Tuesday November 3

☂ The Sultan of Brunei, the world's richest man, pays a state visit to Britain. He and his entourage of 20 will stay at Buckingham Palace (600 rooms). His own palace has 1800 rooms including 275 bathrooms.

Wednesday November 4

☂ Bill Clinton is elected president of the USA. President Bush concedes at 4.15am.

☂ Australian prime minister Paul Keating wins the title of Australia's most offensive politician calling his opponents swill, incompetents, fools and constitutional vandals.

Thursday November 5

☂ Guy Fawkes Night.

☂ Elton John gets a £26million advance from Time Warner Inc for the sole right to market all his music from 1974 and his next 4 albums.

☂ Bobby Fischer (US) wins the two-month $5 million revenge chess match with Boris Spassky (RUS) in Belgrade. They last met in 1972 when Fischer also won.

Friday November 6

☂ Giant panda Lin Lin (7) arrives from Peking as a partner for Tokyo Zoo's Tong Tong, to mark 20yrs of friendship between China and Japan.

☂ An RAF helicopter with a 682lt bucket, which it fills in the Mediterranean, helps to put out forest fires in the mountains SE of Beirut.

Saturday November 7

☂ Wensleydale cheese is to be made in Wensleydale again, where it had been produced from medieval times until last August when Dairycrest closed the creamery.

☂ Indian chief Ben Nighthorse Campbell, becomes the first native American to be elected to the US senate since 1929.

Sunday November 8

☂ Nigel Mansell's car is hit from behind by Ayrton Senna while leading the Australian Grand Prix, and both of them are eliminated from the race. It is Nigel Mansell's last appearance in Formula 1 racing.

Monday November 9

☂ Jodi Evan (24) a (female) member of Canada's Olympic basketball squad and a Rhodes scholar, is banned from Oxford University men's team because the British Universities Sports Federation policy is for single-sex teams.

Tuesday November 10

☂ Ranulph Fiennes and Dr Michael Stroud, set out on their unsupported crossing of Antarctica to raise £2 million for Multiple Sclerosis.

Wednesday November 11

☂ The Synod of the Church of England agrees to the ordination of women.

☂ A Gallup Poll spelling test shows that one in ten of the adults who took it failed to provide a single correct answer. The words are: necessary, accommodation, sincerely, business, separate and height.

Thursday November 12

☂ Five French students cross to England through the Channel Tunnel for a bet. They enter a ventilation shaft at 3.15am, walk 29km in 8hrs, undetected, and cross to the British side where they are taken by the police for questioning. They are returned to France by ferry.

Friday November 13

☂ The Rolling Stones give a 25th anniversary party in New York.

☂ Officials at Chichester, W Sussex, have bought 3000 jars of sausage skins to use as a protective coating for ancient documents in the county's archives.

☂ Pop musician Sting is made an honorary Doctor of Music at Northumbria University, Newcastle-upon-Tyne.

Saturday November 14

In the first rugby international between England and S Africa for 23yrs, England beat S Africa 33-16.

Today is the 70th anniversary of radio broadcasting by the BBC. The first news bulletin was broadcast from the Marconi Building in the Strand, London, at 6pm on November 14, 1922.

Sunday November 15

Harrods is to build a 141 suite hotel opposite its Knightsbridge shop.

Letters from the Earl of Essex to Queen Elizabeth I are expected to sell for £450,000 at Sotheby's on December 14.

Monday November 16

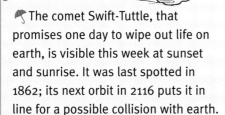

The comet Swift-Tuttle, that promises one day to wipe out life on earth, is visible this week at sunset and sunrise. It was last spotted in 1862; its next orbit in 2116 puts it in line for a possible collision with earth.

Tuesday November 17

Superman, also known as Clark Kent, is dead at the hands of Doomsday, the 2.29m arch villain.

The Queen appoints Dame Ninette de Valois and Sir Michael Aliyah, President of the Royal Society, to the Order of Merit.

Wednesday November 18

Eric Lawes (70), looking for some lost tools with his metal detector in a field at Hoxne, nr. Eye, Suffolk, finds a crumbling chest full of thousands of Roman gold and silver coins, jewellery, ornaments and spoons. A coroner will hold a treasure trove inquest. It is thought to be one of the most important finds ever made in Britain.

England beat Turkey 4-0 and move to second place in the World Cup Qualifying Championship.

Thursday November 19

Two Japanese enamel vases bought for 50p at a village fete sell for £19,800 at Sotheby's.

Britain wins 2 gold and 1 silver medal at the *European Gastronomic Games* in Barcelona. John Burton Race and his team win golds for grouse with salsify and crème brulée (burnt cream) and silver for their oyster and salmon starter.

Friday November 20

A raging fire at Windsor Castle wrecks the state apartments.

This year's Biggest Liar in the World competition, which has been held at Waisdale, Cumbria for more than a century, is won by Derek Martin, a retired aircraft inspector.

Saturday November 21

The royal art collection at Windsor Castle has been saved from the fire because many of the rooms had been emptied the day before for renovation work.

Divers working on a marine survey for the Devon Wildlife Trust find a 20m reef of sunset coral 3km off Lyme Regis.

Sunday November 22

Two cameramen are trapped inside Kilavea volcano on Hawaii when their helicopter crashes. Rescue attempts are hampered by fog and rain.

Monday November 23

Nissan become the first Japanese car manufacturing company to win Europe's Car of the Year Award with its Micra.

Tuesday November 24

The Queen at the 40th anniversary lunch given by the Lord Mayor of London at the Guildhall, speaks about the disasters of 1992 making the year her *'annus horribilis'*.

Wednesday November 25

Cecilia Battistello, managing director of Contship Containers, takes delivery of a 23,000 tonne container ship painted pink. She has plans to have four other new ships painted indigo and turquoise.

The two cameramen trapped inside Kilavea volcano in Hawaii are rescued by helicopter.

Thursday November 26

It is the 41st anniversary of Agatha Christie's play *The Mousetrap*: more than 9.5 million people have seen it so far.

Books, tapes and records worth £116,000 have been returned to Derbyshire libraries during a 2 week amnesty.

Friday November 27

National Tree Week.

The Royal Jubilee Trust plants 40 trees in Hyde Park to celebrate the 40th anniversary of the Queen's reign. Thousands of groups of 40 trees will be planted nationwide.

Saturday November 28

Desert Orchid, the nation's favourite racehorse is making a good recovery from an operation. He has received hundreds of 'get well' cards, including one from the Queen Mother.

Sunday November 29

The Queen moves back into Windsor Castle.

Maureen Lipman wins the Bafta Best TV Actress award for Beattie in the BT ad. Rowan Atkinson wins Best TV Actor for the Barclaycard ad.

The Tomb of King Tutankhamen is opened for two months to celebrate the 70th anniversary of its discovery.

Monday November 30

French police arrest a former convict who held up a post office in Buglose last week and stole Fr47,000 (£5,600) to buy himself a car so that he would no longer have to make his getaways on a bicycle.

The R Severn bursts its banks causing widespread flooding. It's been the wettest November in Wales for 22yrs, with 150mm of rain on Sunday night alone.

December

The separation of the Prince and Princess of Wales is announced

Tuesday December 1

🎄 International Motorbike Show opens in Birmingham; both Norton and Triumph are showing. In the 1950's, 2 out of 3 motorbikes in the world were British made.

🎄 The first British Sign Language Dictionary is published.

🎄 10,000 hectares of the Wash - sand banks, open water, mud flats and marshes - become a National Nature Reserve dedicated to the memory of Sir Peter Scott.

Wednesday December 2

🎄 Eleven rivers are on red alert in S Wales. 3000 tonnes of slurry from a disused coalmine cascade down into the grounds of Tredegar Comp School and stop within metres of the classrooms.

🎄 Lego buys Windsor Safari Park and plans to open a theme park by 1996.

Thursday December 3

🎄 Two IRA bombs disrupt the centre of Manchester: 64 people are injured.

🎄 RSPB buys 121.2 hectares of inter-tidal mud, sand and salt marsh on the Hayle estuary, Cornwall from Sir Peter de Savary for a nominal £1. 343 species of bird have been seen there.

Friday December 4

🎄 The official report blames the Windsor Castle fire on a spotlight accidentally setting fire to a curtain.

Saturday December 5

🎄 Charlton Athletic FC returns to The Valley ground after 7yrs (2627 days).

🎄 Paul Merton is voted Britain's top TV comedy personality. He gained 37% of the 250,000 votes cast.

Sunday December 6

🎄 Hundreds of twitchers descend on South Woodham Ferrers, Essex, to see a rare barbed warbler, only to find it has been eaten by a cat.

🎄 Fake snow is provided to complete the scene at the Victorian weekend at Rochester, Kent.

Monday December 7

🎄 Pop singer Lisa Stanfield wins a court action to ban the release of recordings she made 10yrs ago. Sovereign Music wants to issue an album containing 14 tracks she regards as embarrassing.

Tuesday December 8

🎄 The Worldwide Fund for Nature says British woodlands are being stripped of up to £2 million of bluebells and snowdrops a year to supply garden centres.

🎄 Scottish fishermen block the port of Lochinver, trapping a French trawler, in protest against EEC fishing quotas.

Wednesday December 9

🎄

🎄 Total eclipse of the moon tonight is visible across Europe between 11.07pm and 00.21am.

🎄 Buckingham Palace announces the separation of the Prince and Princess of Wales.

🎄 *Home Alone 2: Lost for Christmas* starring Macaulay Culkin, opens.

Thursday December 10

🎄 An IRA bomb blast at Wood Green Shopping Centre, London injures 101 people.

🎄 Blood given by the Duke of Edinburgh has provided evidence that the bones being examined by forensic experts in London are those of the Russian royal family murdered in 1917.

Friday December 11

🎄 The EEC summit opens at Holyroodhouse Palace, Edinburgh.

🎄 100 rare parrots, smuggled into Europe over the last 5yrs in banana boats docking in Antwerp, are flown back to Colombia in an international rescue operation. Most of them will be returned to the wild.

Saturday December 12

🎄 The Princess Royal marries Commander Tim Laurence in Crathie Church, Balmoral.

🎄 Thousands march in Edinburgh demanding a Scottish Parliament.

Sunday December 13

🎄 An earthquake hits the island of Flores in Indonesia measuring 6.8 on the Richter scale: 1232 people killed.

🎄 Gardners can now buy elephant manure by mail from Chester Zoo for £3 per 13.6kg bag.

Monday December 14

🎄 At the Sportsmen and Women of the Year Awards, Linford Christie is

voted sportsman of the year followed by Nigel Mansell and Nick Faldo. Sally Gunnell is sportswoman of the year, followed by golfer Laura Davis and hockey player Jane Sixsmith.

🎄 Scientists at the University of Wales have discovered how to turn straw into clingfilm.

Tuesday December 15

🎄 Author Ian Fleming's private file on James Bond 007, is sold at Sotheby's for £14,300 to the author's nephew and nieces.

🎄 Hoover is besieged by customers when they offer 2 free flights to the USA to anyone who buys a vacuum cleaner or other electrical equipment for over £100.

Wednesday December 16

🎄 Thousands of Christmas shoppers are evacuated when the IRA plant bombs in Oxford Street, London.

🎄 Norma Major presents the Children of Courage awards, including one to Rachel Lambert (7) who braved a rottweiler's attack to save her brother, at Westminster Cathedral, followed by a tour of No 10 Downing Street .

Thursday December 17

🎄 The ultimate Christmas present, a 14.5kg solid gold Father Christmas and sleigh worth £400,000, goes on show at a Bond Street jewellers.

🎄 200 relics rescued from the *Titanic* by a French salvage team 5yrs ago are being offered for sale by the French government to survivors and descendants of the victims.

Friday December 18

🎄 For the first time, a team from St Thomas's Hospital reveal the secrets of Jeni, an Egyptian mummy (1085-945 BC), without having to remove it from its case and unwrap it. The mummy is scanned and the scans converted into 3D images.

Saturday December 19

🎄 The Twelve Days of Christmas - all the gifts in the song - would cost £10,185 this year.

Sunday December 20

🎄 Shops open for Christmas shopping despite the Sunday trading laws.

🎄 Some American shopping malls are banning the Salvation Army ringing bells while they collect for charity because it disturbs the shoppers. One volunteer in Dallas, Texas fights back by holding a table tennis bat in each hand marked *ding* and *dong*.

Monday December 21

🎄 Peter Robinson, Britain's loneliest lighthouse keeper at Bishop Rock lighthouse, Scilly Isles, comes back to land, as from today the lighthouse is automated.

🎄 Leonie Alderman (21) has become Network Southeast's youngest female train driver.

Tuesday December 22

🎄 The British toy makers Hasbro agree to change Sindy's face as American toy makers Mattell say she looks just like Barbie. Sindy's annual sales are worth $7 million.

🎄 Spain's lottery pays out £812 million - £1.6 million to 95 winners, and £85 to King Juan Carlos: a friend sends him ticket no.00000 every year.

Wednesday December 23

🎄 The RSPCA has stopped finding homes for the animals in their care, in an attempt to prevent impluse giving of puppies and kittens for Christmas.

Thursday December 24

🎄 ▨▨▨▨▨

🎄 Christmas Eve.

🎄 Nigel Mansell will start his career in Indycar racing for Newman-Haas next year driving a Lola made in the UK and costing $200.000.00.

Friday December 25

🎄 Christmas Day

🎄 Crisis at Christmas operates mobile units for the first time offering hamburgers, sausages, beans - and

haircuts - to those who do not want to come into their shelters. The most expensive Christmas lunch in London costs £125 per person at the Savoy Hotel.

🎄 Writer Monica Dickens (77) dies.

Saturday December 26

🎄 Boxing Day.

🎄 Only 5 race meetings take place because of the freezing weather.

Sunday December 27

🎄 DJ Alan Freeman signs off for good from his Radio One programme *'Pick of the Pops'*.

🎄 A £50,000 bridge is to be built for red squirrels when a dual carriageway is built on the Southport-Liverpool road at Ince Blundell, cutting through a wood.

Monday December 28

🎄 Shops report the most hectic start to the sales for years.

🎄 Start of the Hastings International Chess Tournament. The oldest traditional tournament in the world, it has been going since 1895.

Tuesday December 29

🎄 Otters have repopulated 80% of the R Torridge in Devon, the last stronghold of otters in England, and the setting for Henry Williamson's classic tale *Tarka the Otter*. There are thought to be only 15,000 otters left in the UK

Wednesday December 30

🎄 The RSPCA say that more unwanted animals have been abandoned this year than ever before, though Battersea Dogs Home say that they have taken in 13,000 dogs this year, 1,500 fewer than last year.

Thursday December 31

🎄 A thousand beacons are lit across Europe to mark the arrival of the Single European Market. Prime Minister John Major lights the first beacon in the UK in the City of London on the stroke of midnight.

🎄 Britain hands over the presidency of the EEC to Denmark.